OUR CUSTOMERS, OUR FRIENDS

WHAT 50 YEARS IN BUSINESS HAS TAUGHT RITA AND RICK CASE ABOUT SALES SUCCESS AND COMMUNITY SERVICE

RICK CASE

A Smart Business Network Inc. imprint

Published by Smart Business Network Inc.

Cover design by Scott Eble

Layout and design by Jim Mericsko

Edited by Dustin S. Klein

ISBN 13: 978-0-9839983-1-0

Contents

Foreword

By H. Wayne Huizenga

The first time I met Rick and Rita Case, I remember being impressed with the energy of their personalities. They are such outgoing people, always talking and making connections. They are in your face all the time — in a good way. You'll walk away thinking, "Those are good people. If I'm going to buy a car, I'm going to buy one from them."

Rick and Rita are always working, even at social events. It's hard to draw the line where their business lives end and their personal lives begin because they are all about the business, all the time. I admire the wonderful work ethic they share. They don't slack off at all. They're constantly on the lookout for new opportunities. And they do a heck of a job following through to make the most of those opportunities.

Even though I founded AutoNation, which is Rick's big competitor, I have nothing but good things to say about the man. The Cases have built a good organization that's well respected — even by their biggest competitors.

There are a lot of car dealerships around, but some just perform better than others. That's because those dealers have figured how to innovate to stay ahead of the competition in every aspect of their business. That's Rick Case. He's a quarter step ahead on the financing side, a half step ahead on the sales side, and three-quarters of a step ahead on the service side. Innovation is a matter of asking how much better you can be at each thing you do. That's the key to being successful and staying in business and growing.

And the special thing about Rick and Rita is that they work just as hard for nonprofit organizations as they do for their own business. They put a lot of time into organizations like the Boys & Girls Clubs. I don't know how they keep that up, but they deserve two gold medals for it.

Most of the time when I see Rick, it's at some kind of a fundraising event. He's always involved. Rick and Rita don't just write a check and sit back. They write a check and they're involved in making it happen, just like they get involved and make things happen for their own business. Between the two of them, boy, they've got a ton of energy. There's no stopping them.

"Entrepreneurialism is an artistic characteristic. If you talk about an artist, they start with a blank canvas. There's nothing on it. And all of a sudden, they see something others do not and create something remarkable that someone else can't. Entrepreneurs are the artists of the business world, or the blank space. There's nothing happening and an entrepreneur comes along and says, 'Aha! I see how to make this magic happen.' And they bring it about. So it's about creativity in business; it's an artistic ability. And Rick Case has that — he has it in spades."

— Mike Jackson, chairman and CEO of AutoNation,
the largest car retailer in America

Introduction

"Hi, I'm Rick Case."

This line became iconic as the opening to my radio and TV commercials that started back in the 1960s. And now, 50 years later, I'll often revert to that line when I meet with business executives or wealthy philanthropists. I'll say, "Hi, I'm Rick Case. I'm a car salesman from Akron, Ohio."

Before I grew into any of the titles people often assign to me — like car dealer, promoter, entrepreneur, pioneer, philanthropist, or marketing guru — I was just a car salesman from Akron with a big dream. I started out with the goal of being the best so I could sell the most. What began with the sale of a used car from my parents' driveway in Akron, Ohio, when I was 14, and then with my first dealership in 1962, has grown into the Rick Case Auto Group, which today operates 15 dealerships in three states with 1,000 employees, generating more than a half a billion dollars in sales every year. We hold the United States all-time one-month volume sales records for Fiat, Acura, and Honda cars, as well as Honda motorcycles.

Throughout the 50-year history of the Rick Case Auto Group, I have learned a lot about what it takes to become the best and stay on top — and I continue learning new things every day. When an industry changes as much as the automotive industry has during the past half century, you have to be open to learning new lessons in order to thrive. Through the pages of this book, I'll share the lessons I've learned while navigating the highs and lows of this business.

All the while, my persistence and passion have been constant. I had the burning desire to be No. 1, and that fueled me along the journey. Because I believed I could achieve my goal, nothing could stand in my way. "No" was not an answer I would accept, because entrepreneurs can always find a way to make things happen — even if they have to overcome several obstacles to do it.

Believe me, there are a lot of obstacles to overcome when you build a business as a pioneer, innovating and introducing new products and ideas before anyone else. But we've never been afraid to be first. We've built an unmatched reputation for successfully pioneering import car brands never sold in the United States — including Toyota in 1966, Fiat in 1970 (and again when the brand returned to America in 2011), Honda in 1972, Lancia in 1975, Isuzu in 1982, Acura and Hyundai in 1986, Mitsubishi in 1988, Kia in 1995, and smart car in 2008.

Part of our success has come from our decisions about which cars to carry at our dealerships. But I can't rely on our products being better because other dealers sell Audi, Acura, Fiat, Honda, Hyundai, Kia, Mazda, and Mitsubishi, too. The differentiation comes from the dealer. Customers are willing to switch brands to do business with dealers they like.

My career has never been about innovating for the sake of innovation or pioneering just for the sake of being first or promoting crazy ideas just for the sake of a catchy ad. All of my ideas are designed with the customer in mind. Everything ties back to our core philosophy of treating our customers as we would treat our best friends. That treatment — combined with the best guarantees in the industry, like doubling all of the factory warranties, as well as our Customer Rewards Card Program with discount gas and free carwashes for life — that's the secret to our success. We deliver value that customers can't get anywhere else, and that's why they choose Rick Case over competitors and keep coming back to buy again.

Staying at the top of your field isn't easy. It takes hard work, long hours, and creative problem solving. It takes risk to do what's never been done before and to try ideas that our competitors call "crazy."

But that's what it takes to be a successful entrepreneur. It requires the highest level of work ethic, innovation, and commitment to develop and execute the ideas that solve problems in record-setting ways.

Those skills aren't just restricted to business. I have found — and created — opportunities to apply this same set of entrepreneurial skills to the world of philanthropy to make a much larger impact on our community than I ever could with a car business. The passion, hard work, commitment, and creativity that made the Rick Case Auto Group successful are now also focused on charities like the Boys & Girls Clubs, which help provide better futures to less fortunate children. Our events have raised more than $50 million for the Boys & Girls Clubs alone.

You'll find that the lessons that have paved the way for the 50-year legacy of Rick Case aren't only applicable to the automobile industry. These are ideas that play a vital role in any type of business — and beyond, in any type of philanthropy. We invite you to join with us in celebrating 50 years of success at the Rick Case Auto Group by taking a peek into some of the lessons and events that have made us so successful in our communities.

Rick Case "on the air," recording his famous "Hi. This is Rick Case" radio spots and working as a DJ at a radio station, 1974

Chapter 1

Lesson #1: If you want to succeed, you'll overcome anything

Whenever people ask me what I do, I tell them I'm a car salesman. Not a car dealer or a businessman, or anything like that. A car salesman. But before I discovered my calling, I was just a salesman.

I was always interested in cars, even as a kid. But I was more interested in selling stuff and making money. When I was 6 years old, I made potholders and sold those. I picked strawberries at my uncle's farm and horseradish along the railroad tracks and sold those along the road. I sold newspapers at a corner grocery store, too.

Then, when I was 9 years old, I got a paper delivery route. The same route day after day wasn't enough for me, so I took on additional routes and hired other boys to make the deliveries for me. I made more money than any other delivery boy that way, and I didn't even have to ride through the rain to do it. I even saved up enough money to buy my first boat: a 12-foot Yellowjacket.

When I was in school, I never ate lunch because I was selling. While the other kids had lunch, I'd set up shop at my locker to sell gum and candy I bought wholesale from a distributor. I was skipping lunch to sell, but even then, I didn't have a vision for the future or plans for what I wanted to be when I grew up.

That is, until I sold my first car.

When I was 14, I bought an old Ford. I fixed it up and sold it from the driveway of my parents' home in Akron, Ohio, for a profit of $400. I made more money on that one car than I made on my paper route in a whole year. And that was it. I knew what I wanted to do with my life.

To many people today, cars are just basic transportation. But you have to remember that back in the 1950s, cars were a big deal. After World War II and through the '60s, cars changed dramatically every year, so everyone's attention was on them, waiting to see what was next. People wanted to get a different car every year or two, whether it was brand new or used. If you had a two-year-old car, your car was aged because the new cars coming out every year looked so different. People wanted to keep up with their neighbors, so they would buy a new car — or a newer used car — every year or two.

Because of this trend, I found it pretty easy to sell cars. So I bought and sold another car and another and another, until I eventually ended up with a small used car lot.

It was an old used car lot that probably hadn't been used in years. It was just this small building, maybe 10-feet-by-10-feet, right across the street from the B.F. Goodrich Tire & Rubber Co. factory. Rent was $25 a month. The name — Moxie Motors — came from MAD Magazine because I was still a teenager. I had read those growing up and thought naming my business after something I'd seen in MAD Magazine would be neat.

Then, because I had a building and an address, I could send in my application for a dealer license. With that, I could not only sell cars retail but also wholesale, which I did a lot of in the early days. I would buy cars, recondition them, and then resell them to other dealers at auctions.

What was it about selling cars? I guess it was the money — and the fun. When you find something that's fun for you, you're usually more successful at it than if you don't enjoy your job at all — even if that job makes you a lot of money. When you don't like what you do, you won't want to work hard at it. And if you don't work hard at it, chances are you will not be good at it.

For me, it was always about being the best. And when you want to be the best, you find ways to do things that other people can't or won't. I wanted to be the best car salesman there was. But back in those days, good role models in that industry were hard to find. So for me to be the best, I literally had to do what no one else was doing.

I was still in high school when I started going to dealer auto auctions. Nobody respected me. In fact, a lot of them wanted to take advantage of me. This was back when car salesmen were earning bad reputations. After the war in the late '40s and '50s, there were 50,000 car dealers — so many of them that there weren't enough cars to go around and keep up with the huge demand. Each dealer would receive only 20 or 30 cars a month, more demand than supply. The dealers would take advantage of customers by overcharging them. That's why Congress passed the Automobile Information Disclosure Act in 1958 that required every new car to have the Monroney sticker affixed to the window, giving customers information about the Manufacturer's Suggested Retail Price (MSRP), engine and transmission specifications, warranty information, and other details.

The industry was made up of a lot of outlaws — unethical dealers and dishonest salespeople — and I was just a kid among them. The odds were stacked against me. At the auctions, older guys would call me "The White Socks Kid" because only kids wore white socks at that time. Because I'd already made up my mind that car sales were going to be my career, I decided that nothing — not these guys or anyone else — would stand in my way. I learned my first business lesson then: It's all about how much you really want to win. If your desire is to be successful, you'll find a way to overcome anything.

The dealers and salesmen at the auctions wouldn't respect me because I was a kid. So I decided to make myself look older. I began wearing a hat and topcoat, and I started chewing on a cigar. I've never smoked in my life, but I'd chew on cigars just to look older. Despite this, they wouldn't take a check from me, so I had to buy cars with cash.

Unfortunately, there were a lot of shady people in the car business, and a lot of them wanted to take advantage of me — especially when they heard I was paying cash.

These hurdles caused me to mature quickly in business. I realized that I couldn't just look older; I had to be smart, too. A lot of what I learned was self-taught. In Ohio at that time, the car dealerships were only open Monday and Thursday nights. So after I got my license, on Monday and Thursday nights I would drive to the local dealerships and sit with the used car managers. I got them to like me by treating them right. You get people to like you by being fair, honest, and ethical with them.

When people like you, they will help you. So by taking this approach with the dealership managers, I started to build relationships with them where they would let me watch and learn, giving me quick lessons on how to inspect cars for damage and how to watch for odometers being turned back. From them, I learned how to appraise a car. Then, when their dealerships would get busy, they'd ask me to help out and appraise cars. I'd even end up buying cars from them to resell, either on my lot or to other dealers.

Sometimes, I learned the hard way. I made mistakes, too, which always helps the learning process. When appraising a car, I'd sometimes fail to notice a bad transmission or a bad motor. I would end up losing money on those mistakes, spending money to fix those cars so I could sell them. Or, when I'd go sell a car at an auction, dealers would detect that it had been in an accident, and again, I would lose money on those cars. Early on, I learned there was no faster way to learn than to lose money.

From being around dealers and salespeople who gave the industry a bad name, I learned a lot of what not to do. But I didn't let any of them stand in my way of succeeding in the car business. After a while — with my hat, cigar, white socks, honesty, ethics, and all of the lessons learned from on-the-job-training at dealerships — I finally earned their respect.

In 1964, after Moxie Motors, I opened a bigger used car lot called Sharp Used Cars in Barberton, a suburb of Akron. This was a real used car lot, with 30 cars on it. It had a garage where I'd fix and clean the cars myself. I also did all of the selling, all of the bookkeeping, and all of the financing. I did it all; I was a one-man show. Like I had in high school, I was selling straight through meals without stopping to eat. That worried my mother, who thought I was not eating enough, and she would bring meals to me at the dealership.

Around that time, color TVs were just coming out. Everybody wanted one. It was the post-war car craze all over again, so I jumped in that business, too, and opened a store called Color City TV in a nearby shopping center. I understood the power of entertainment as a sales tool, and I put radio station disc jockeys in each window at the front of the store, where they would broadcast live to draw people in. Inside the store, I had television sets stacked to the ceiling — Motorola, RCA, and a lot of names that aren't around anymore. And I would sell tons of TVs.

Looking back over the past half-century, I've realized that I just hit the ground running as a kid without really ever having a regular job. I have always worked for myself in some way — always a salesman and entrepreneur. What I've learned is actually pretty simple and straightforward. The key to success boils down to controlling your own destiny and not being at the mercy of others. Of course, it helped that I got behind products as soon as they came out, hoping they would be hot and in high demand. But, I think my passion and commitment to succeed were more important than the product itself. Being your own boss isn't always the easiest path, that's for sure. I made my share of mistakes and learned many things the hard way. Once you've set a goal, you just can't take the easy way out or give up when the odds stack against you. If you've made up your mind to be the biggest, you have to be the best first. To achieve that goal, you must find a way to overcome everything. That has become the story of my life.

First Rick Case dealership Moxie Motors, 1962, Akron, Ohio

Rick Case high school photo, 1960

Second Rick Case dealership Sharp Used Cars, 1964, Barberton, Ohio

Chapter 2

Lesson #2: Don't take no for an answer

It was 1964 when I heard that Honda had started making cars in Japan. I'd seen what the company had done with motorcycles and how it had created a market where there really wasn't one. Harley Davidson was struggling, selling next to nothing back in those years. Then Honda came along in 1959 and created a market for the "Nifty Thrifty Honda-Fifty," and things changed. Honda's entrance into the marketplace re-energized the industry. Honda's first ads claimed, "You meet the nicest people on a Honda."

I figured if Honda could do this with a motorcycle, it would do well with a car. I thought, "Well, I've got to get in on the ground floor of this." This gave me a very specific goal to chase: I wanted to be the first Honda motorcycle dealer considered when Honda brought its first car to the U.S. market.

In 1965, I submitted my application and received a Honda motorcycle franchise in Wooster, Ohio — the closest place to my hometown that I could open a dealership where there wasn't one already. That officially made me a motorcycle dealer, but remember, I was on a quest to become a new car dealer. By then, I had become pretty good at selling used cars — I had even started selling some from the Honda motorcycle dealership in Wooster — but I didn't have any new car experience.

Then Toyota came along, the first Japanese automobile to hit the U.S. "Maybe," I thought, "I'll look even better in Honda's eyes when its cars come here if I have experience pioneering another imported car." So I went to the distributor in Chicago to see if I could get Toyota in my motorcycle dealership.

As a motorcycle dealer, I was a unique case for Toyota because I'd be putting its car in a motorcycle dealership. On top of that, the dealership was in Wooster, Ohio, and Toyota wasn't ready to head into a market that small.

I showed Toyota my successful track record so far of selling everything from motorcycles to color TVs — of course, putting the emphasis on my used car experience and success. I focused on figures, such as how many used cars I had sold in Barberton, which was more than any other new or used car dealer in all of Summit County. Because all four years of my career so far had been spent selling cars — and successfully, at that — Toyota felt confident giving one of its first car franchises to a motorcycle dealer in Wooster, Ohio. So in 1966, Toyota cars came to my Honda motorcycle dealership, making it the first new car franchise I ever had.

In 1967, I opened another Honda motorcycle dealership in Barberton, Ohio. That was the first one that featured my name: Rick Case Honda. Soon after, I opened one in Cuyahoga Falls, just north of Akron. A third location, near Kent State University, followed after that. In a year's time, we had grown from three employees to more than 25. As we grew, Honda executives took notice. They couldn't believe how many motorcycles I was selling from these dealerships — more than 100 a month. Whenever I asked them to open a dealership, they let me do it. I was on a roll.

Still, every time I would see my Honda motorcycle representative, I'd ask him when the car was coming. My goal was to end up with the car dealerships, and selling motorcycles had become a means to reach that goal. I knew that in order to achieve my goals, I had to be successful with what I was given. Only then would Honda — and others — let me represent their brands of automobiles.

So I just started selling everything. It was really pretty simple; it came down to knowing who I was selling to and giving them what they wanted. Those days, young kids from 16 to 25 were the ones buying motorcycles, so I thought about ways to sell to them. Whatever approach I tried, it was always based around the customer.

Then I thought of a new idea: Who else could be my customer?

Back then, you didn't have to have a license in Ohio to drive a moped because the engines were under 50ccs. That meant my customer demographic didn't have to start at age 16. And what better way to appeal to younger customers than with lower prices.

I started advertising a layaway plan — the first that I know of — that allowed this younger demographic to buy a moped for $3 a week or $9.95 a month. Any kid could make $3 a week from a paper route or by mowing lawns, and every kid wanted a moped.

We sold thousands of mopeds and quickly became the largest moped dealer in the world — because most motorcycle dealers did not realize this opportunity to market the 50cc vehicles to kids under age 16. Nobody else thought that if you finance mopeds for the smaller pocketbooks of 14- and 15-year-olds, that you could essentially create a new, captive audience.

Then, I thought, why not go after even younger customers? I could start them out on bicycles, then take them up to a 10-speed, then a moped to prime them for scooters to, ultimately, help them grow into motorcycles. At that time, bikes — like cars and color TVs — were a big deal, so they easily drew in kids as young as 6 or 7. I even went to Taiwan to manufacture our own Rick Case brand of 10-speed bicycles. Later, I became the U.S. distributor of a French 10-speed bike brand called St. Etienne. In those days, the 10-speed bike was the top of the line. I don't know if it was just hot at the time or if I helped make it hot, but I do know that no other motorcycle or car dealers thought to sell the whole spectrum of bikes from their dealerships. They only sold cars or only sold motorcycles. I made my store a family affair, where kids could grow up buying from Rick Case.

I had the low-end bikes to compete with Sears and Montgomery Ward, and I had the high-end bikes to compete with the sophisticated bicycle shops. Because I was selling so many different products, I started bringing in customers of all ages. When you sell more types of products that appeal to more types of people, you bring in a lot more people. No matter what I sold, I outsold everybody, even the big box retailers like Children's Palace.

At one time, in my Cuyahoga Falls dealership, I sold three brands of cars, three brands of bicycles, six brands of mopeds, Vespa motor scooters, Skidoo and Arctic Cat snowmobiles, and four brands of motorcycles: Kawasaki, Honda, Yamaha, and Suzuki. Because I was selling such a variety, I could charge lower prices all around and still turn a profit. Except for cars regulated by law, the more products I bought from a supplier, the lower price I could negotiate, therefore I could sell for less.

While people called me crazy for advertising such low prices, I was really creating a win-win because I was getting what I wanted — selling more products — and my customers were getting what they wanted — affordable transportation. I would advertise crazy prices because I knew the more I could sell, the lower prices I could offer. The reality was that I was just trying to sell as much stuff as I could, as fast as I could to get as many customers as possible, of all ages, accustomed to buying at Rick Case, so when I got the Honda car I would have a huge customer base to sell them to.

Next, I got into snow blowers when they first came out. This was before snow blowers were a staple to surviving the harsh Northeast Ohio winters. People didn't know if they would actually use them, so I would do crazy things to make their purchasing decision easier.

I would advertise, "If we don't get 50 inches of snow this winter, I'll buy your snow blower back from you for what you paid for it."

People thought I was crazy for offering this deal. Maybe I was. But thanks to Northeast Ohio's weather, we almost always had more than 50 inches of snow. I never had to buy back a snow blower.

Despite the reputation, all the crazy things I did were based around the customer. Everything I did was good for them. My logic was simple: I would ask myself, "How can I eliminate the risk of buying a snow blower? How can I create a deal around this bicycle?" Other dealers wouldn't even think about doing things like that. Or if they did think about doing it after they saw me do it, they were too nervous of the risk to do it themselves.

I thought differently than most dealers about risk. Other dealers would think, "What if there wasn't 50 inches of snow and I have to buy every snow blower back? That's too big a risk to take." I would think, "What are the chances of there not being 50 inches of snow based on the facts of historical data and then if there was an usually light snow fall, less than 50 inches, how many people would actually bring back a snow blower they know is a useful tool they could use for years to come?" To me it was no risk, and I would sell hundreds of snow blowers with this promotion.

Through it all, I was driven to sell more than anybody else. I needed to keep the momentum going if I was going to earn the car dealerships from Honda. I never had any plan to remain a motorcycle dealer. I only wanted to get in on the ground floor of Honda's cars, and I had to start selling a bunch of motorcycles to get there. Still, my passion was the car business, so I started looking for other opportunities to bring in cars while I waited on Honda.

Fiat had been in the country a few years by then. When I went after the franchise in 1970, my success selling new Toyota cars was enough to prove my capability, and Fiat awarded me its car franchise in three of my motorcycle dealerships. That was the same year I became the first Midwest distributor for Lamborghini. After several days of negotiating with the exotic brand's factory people at the New York Auto Show, they agreed and sold me some cars on the spot.

Honda first showed its car in the United States at the Chicago Auto Show in 1969. There was only one Honda factory rep there — Cliff Schmillen, who 20 years later became the top American executive at Honda. I was the only one there with him, working Honda's display booth. During the show, the organizers secretly stop by each manufacturer's booth to see how well representatives were presenting their products. There's a contest for the person who does the best job of explaining a new product, and I was selected as the winner.

Then came the event I'd been waiting for. Five years after I got my first Honda motorcycle franchise, Honda finally introduced its cars to the United States. The first Honda car franchises went to 30 Honda motorcycle dealers in California in 1970. The very first dealership went to Bill and Lori Manly in Santa Rosa, a successful Honda motorcycle dealer and a family I'll end up getting to know very well in the next decade.

Honda was assigning the car franchise and selling the Honda cars first on the west coast, where their national office was located. Slowly they moved east, and finally, after a year, Honda was in the Midwest to select its Honda car dealers. By that time, Honda had established an Auto division separate from the motorcycle division. American Honda hired an experienced automotive executive to head up the car division and he didn't want anything to do with the motorcycle division or its dealers. He felt the best dealers to market the Honda car were experienced, established new automobile dealers in their current market. He told his auto division, "All right, no more motorcycle dealers get the car." Honda changed its rule of cars only going to motorcycle dealers and said it wouldn't give the car to any motorcycle dealers, only existing, experienced new car dealers.

Talk about irony. Here I was with 10 motorcycle dealerships in Cleveland, Akron, Cuyahoga Falls, North Randall, Parma, Wooster, Kent, and Barberton. I had been opening all of these motorcycle dealerships and selling lots of motorcycles because I wanted to get Honda's attention for the car. And here comes the car to the Midwest at last, and Honda won't let me carry it because I'm a motorcycle dealer. Ultimately, the local Honda car franchise was awarded to a Ford dealer in Akron — which was even a bigger insult because it was my hometown.

I still wouldn't take Honda's no for an answer. Then, one of the guiding philosophies of my life kicked in. You're probably already familiar with it if you have kids, who seem to have a knack for nagging their way to anything they want. It has become one of my mottos: Persistence removes resistance. It meant, in the face of any "no," I would never give up. I just kept charging persistently ahead.

I started going to that Akron Honda dealer on a regular basis and bugging him to sell me the franchise. After he had the car franchise for about one year — selling a total of 25 Hondas during the entire year because he wasn't really paying attention to it — I visited him again. This time, I decided I wasn't going to leave until he sold me the Honda car franchise. I ended up buying it for $6,500, including all of the parts and factory signage.

Every time the factory said no, there was always a way to make it happen. I learned a valuable lesson from this experience: Successful entrepreneurs don't take "no" for an answer. They always find a way to make things happen. They keep asking. They keep adjusting. They keep selling. They understand that when they're persistent, they'll remove any resistance keeping them from their goal. And eventually, whatever it is they want will happen.

I wanted to prove something to Honda — that it had made a mistake by not awarding me a dealership in the first place.

I still had to fly out to Los Angeles and meet with Honda executives to sign the dealer agreement. Because the former franchise owner wasn't performing well, the company agreed to make the transfer. When it did, I promised Honda I would become the largest dealer in the country. I took my advertising manager, Ned Tookman, with me on that trip, and we returned together on the red-eye flight to Cleveland, getting into town around 6 a.m. on Saturday morning.

"Why don't you go home and get a good rest over the weekend, and I'll see you on Monday?" I told him.

This is how Tookman tells the rest of the story:

"So I come in Monday morning at 6:30 a.m.. Rick's office was on the second floor, and he had these curtains over the windows that would be open early in the morning, and later in the day, when things got going, he'd close them. I drive into the parking lot, I look up and he's standing in front of the window with this big smile on his face.

"I walk in and see the showroom floor is full of Honda cars. I can't believe what I'm seeing. Rick meets me as I'm coming through the door. I said, 'Rick, where did you get these cars?' And he says, 'I grabbed some of the guys, and we went to Pittsburgh and picked up these cars.'

"Then he said, 'We are going to sell 100 Honda cars this month.' That was his exact comment to me. And all I can remember is I looked at him and I said, 'Yes, we are.' He never took no for an answer, and that's the way he managed. If he thought something could be done, he expected you to think the same way."

What had happened was, after we returned on Saturday morning, I got busy. I started calling car dealers in the area and asking them to sell me some cars because the dealership I bought only had six cars in stock. As many cars as they agreed to sell me, I grabbed that many guys from my dealership — from mechanics to sales associates — and took them to Pittsburgh so they could each drive one back.

Once we had all the cars, selling them was easy. That first month of business — June 1972 — wasn't even a full month, and we still sold 103 new Hondas and became the largest volume dealer in the country. I also became the first Honda dealer in the country to sell more than 100 new Honda cars in one month.

That certainly wasn't the last time I was told no and had to find my own yes. In fact, Honda car dealership No. 2 came with just as much resistance.

By that time, the Rick Case name was really starting to saturate the Cleveland/Akron area, with my Honda motorcycle dealerships scattered from the West side to the East side and south to Barberton, Cuyahoga Falls, Kent, and Wooster. All of these Honda dealerships were in one area, and Honda said I had a monopoly. Before I could open another Honda car dealership in Cleveland, the factory told me I'd need to give up one of the motorcycle stores. I ended up selling the motorcycle store in Barberton to open my second Honda car dealership in Cleveland.

Sometimes it takes negotiation and compromise, but there's a way around every "no."

First Rick Case Honda motorcycle dealership, 1965; first Toyota car dealership, 1966, Wooster, Ohio

Second Rick Case Honda motorcycle dealership, 1968, Barberton, Ohio

Rick Case with a truck load of Honda mini motorcycles, 1971

Rick with Soichiro Honda in Japan, 1968, recognized as the largest volume Honda motorcycle dealer in the U.S.

Honda's first car introduction, the Honda 360, 1969 Chicago Auto Show. (This car was not sold in the U.S. but Honda made its "debut" in the U.S. with this auto show display.)

a dealer's view

he hitched his wagon to a two-wheeled star

Advertising and promotion are building blocks with which the Rick Case empire was constructed. The dynamic motorcycle dealer — and Goodyear motorcycle tire distributor — stands in the showroom of his new million-dollar store.

IF YOU WERE 23 years old, a private businessman earning enough to make ends meet, and you decided to set your goal on becoming a millionaire before age 30, how would you go about achieving that goal?

If the year were 1966 and your name was Rick Case, you would sell your used car business and become a motorcycle dealer.

That's right, a motorcycle dealer.

Today, 29-year-old Rick Case runs a multi-million dollar chain of motorcycle stores, he's the largest motorcycle dealer in the world, and he figures he's on the ground floor of a business skyrocket that's just beginning to lift off.

"You haven't seen anything yet," he asserts, adding that his business has increased by at least 300 per cent each year since 1966.

"And I don't see any reason for that trend to change in the near future," he says.

GO magazine interviewed Case for his views on the motorcycle sport and its future.

He doesn't see any reason for pessimism. "Not in my lifetime, at least," he says.

He sees motorcycle retailing as the fastest-growing industry in the U. S. today.

"One reason lies in the fact that human beings are basically lazy creatures. We seek the easiest solution to our problems.

"The second reason for this growth is the fact that Americans are finding themselves with more and more spare time to fill.

"Enter the motorcycle.

"It's the only sport that requires no advance planning.

"Between the time you leave your job and the time you arrive at home, you can make a

Article about Rick Case

Case has seen his business expand at least 300 per cent annually since its beginning in 1966. His secretary, Hiroko Howard, is his chief schedule-arranger.

a dealer's view

snap decision to go for a bike ride.

"So you hop on your motorcycle and take a half hour ride before dinner.

"In that half hour of fresh air, late afternoon sunshine and what seems like unrestricted freedom, you can achieve a greater degree of relaxation than you could by playing a round of golf, going to a baseball game or spending a day fishing.

"And you don't have to reserve a tee-off time, you don't have to wait 'till you have a day off to go to the game, and you don't have to hunt for a place where the fish are biting.

"You just strap on your helmet, disappear for half an hour and when you sit down at the dinner table you're a new man," he smiles.

Case's current effort is to make 'motorcycle' a household word in his Cleveland-Akron, Ohio metropolitan market area. To do so, he has budgeted half a million dollars for a three-month television campaign.

"We're going to show the public how very special the joys of motorcycling can be."

The Honda-Kawasaki dealer built his empire on just that kind of big-promotion thinking.

"I'm also thinking more and more about my service capabilities," he says. "Now that I have all those bikes on the road (he sold 10,000 units in 1971 alone) I simply cannot afford to let my service departments be anything but top-notch."

Case celebrated the grand opening of two, million-dollar stores in April. One, located in Cleveland, is his seventh outlet. The other, in Cuyahoga Falls, a suburb of Akron, stands on the site of one of his earlier shops.

A look into the service area of the Cuyahoga Falls store reveals that he isn't kidding about attention to service.

He employs 30 mechanics and they work in a spotless, white-paneled and metal-protected service area outfitted with 11 hydraulic lifts for motorcycles.

Case owns a distributing company which supplies all of his retail outlets with parts, accessories and supplies. That company, Associated

Standing in a forest of motorcycles in his service department, Case points to the overhead posters commenting, "Men's liberation, that's where it's at."

Distributing Co., is a franchised Goodyear motorcycle tire distributor.

"The bike tire replacement market already is big business," says Case. "It's certain to grow right along with the whole market.

"One of our bikes, the 750cc Kawasaki, is a notorious tire eater. It's the fastest production motorcycle in the world and when you really turn the power loose, it simply fries the rear tire.

"We've seen the rear tires on these bikes worn smooth in less than 4,000 miles. An average rider will get 5,000 to 6,000 miles per rear tire, and a guy who babies the bike may go 8,000 miles before he buys a new tire.

"But the bike literally begs to be ridden . . . it's so much fun. So the miles roll by in a hurry.

"We move a lot of replacement tires . . . through all seven outlets," he says.

Case predicts his motorcycle unit sales will top the 30,000 mark in 1972. "We have some customers who have eight bikes for a family of five."

"We want more of those families," he says. GO

GO

THE GOODYEAR TIRE DEALER MAGAZINE

May, 1972
Volume 62, Number 5

Published every month for Goodyear dealers and associate dealers in the United States by the publications department of The Goodyear Tire & Rubber Company, Akron, Ohio 44316

Member: International Association of Business Communicators; Akron Chapter, IABC.

Mort Leggett, *publications manager*

Larry D. Miller, *editor*

Mike Starn, *associate editor*

Robert R. Wise, *art director*

The cover: In this issue, GO explores the booming motorcycle market in the United States. To get in the spirit of the sport, Editor Larry Miller raced a unique machine, the Rokon Trail 140, in an Arizona motocross event. Ace rider Ralph Grindstaff of Phoenix demonstrated proper racing style on the RT-140 for this cover shot. A report on the race begins on page two. Photo by Larry Miller.

Chapter 3

Lesson #3: Start early, plan your day, and work your plan

I've always been the first one into the dealership every morning and the last one to leave every night. When I first got into the business those hours were because I had a lot of work to do. In my first couple of dealerships, I wore many hats to handle parts, service, sales, financing, and accounting. Accomplishing all of those tasks required long hours, so I needed to be in the dealership by 5 a.m. and might not leave until 11 p.m.

Since the beginning of my business, 14- and 18-hour workdays and seven-day workweeks have been the norm for me. I started opening my dealerships on Sunday before other dealers did.

As my company grew and I brought on more associates, it became more important than ever to maintain that "first in, last out" schedule. When the leader of a company is the first one into the office every morning, already hard at work when the associates arrive at 8, you really set the example for your people. On the other hand, if the top executive wanders in at 10 after everyone else is in the office, it doesn't set the pace for your people. And, it's harder to gain their respect. The speed of the boss is the speed of the crew.

Leaders should model for their employees what the path to success looks like. And entrepreneurs know from experience that the path is paved with commitment. If any of my associates aspire to sit in my chair one day, they know what it takes. They know they're going to have to work the kind of hours I work to succeed. If your work ethic is to arrive at 9 or 10 a.m. and dart out of the office at 5 p.m., your success will be limited.

When you have passion for what you do — which is another

necessary ingredient for success — you don't feel the clock pulling you away from work. Usually, entrepreneurs arrive at work first because ideas are exploding in their head and they can't wait to get them out and test them. If you really love what you do, that enthusiasm and commitment keeps you focused on working hard when others leave for the day.

That one day in January 1970, by all means, I should have ran out of the dealership. It was a day I still remember like yesterday, but like every other day, my top priority was the work at hand — which, at that moment in time, was to sell a motorcycle to the customer who was standing in front of me at the Barberton store.

At that time, the store had one mechanic in the shop. While I was in the showroom with this customer, the mechanic was filling up a motorcycle with gasoline, and the tank overflowed. The stream ran across the shop floor and under a natural gas-operated hot water heater. The flame from the heater ignited the gasoline stream, and the fire leapt toward the motorcycle.

Realizing what had happened, the mechanic dropped the gas can and sprinted out of the building before the fire reached him.

Of course, I ran the other direction — right into the shop. I wanted to save the motorcycle, so I was going to try to put the fire out.

In the process, I knocked over a can of gas and it spilled all over me. The flames leapt onto me, too, and suddenly, I was on fire.

I managed to escape the building by crawling out of a back window, getting outside where I could quell the fire that was on me. By the time I put it out, I had serious second- and third-degree burns over most of my body — covering my face, chest, arms, and legs. The customer I'd been with didn't leave. He watched what happened and came to my aid. He helped me into his car, with flesh dripping off my body, and drove me to the hospital as fast as he could.

Fortunately, there was a doctor at the hospital who was a burn specialist that had just returned from Vietnam. He immediately took me into emergency surgery, which lasted eight hours, and performed several skin grafts.

By all rights, I should not have been communicating with anyone for weeks. But I didn't have anyone who could run the business and I wasn't going to let being in the hospital affect sales. So the next day, from the intensive care unit, I called my manager at my other store in Kent and asked him to come into the ICU so I could walk him through all of the deals I had been working. I filled him in on all the details so he could temporarily take over for me.

Till this day, I clearly remember my parents standing over me in the hospital, thinking how lucky I was to have survived the fire. And there I was, working on deals, not letting the situation slow down business. I remember telling the manager from Kent the name of the customer who drove me to the hospital so he could follow up to see if he still wanted to buy a motorcycle. I even remember the motorcycle he had been looking at. I don't know how I remember all these details over 40 years later, but that's one day I'll never forget.

Even though I was stuck in the hospital for two more months, undergoing a series of surgeries, I kept working as much as I could. I even made the calls from the hospital to lease a new building to replace the dealership that had burned down.

"Rick enjoys the business a lot," says John Lanigan, a Cleveland radio personality at a station that was an advertising partner of ours. "He has a good time selling cars. Here's a guy who ran back into a burning building to save his motorcycles when he almost lost it all in the very beginning, and got burned over 80 percent of his body in that whole process.

But he wasn't going to let his motorcycles go up in smoke. He really cared about the business and he really wanted to make it work."

That's the thing about true entrepreneurs — they keep working hard, even when it's not easy or convenient, because they're passionate about the business and they really want to succeed. They work hard when others would just lie down and rest. I had a lot of energy, a lot of passion, and I would always find a way to make everything happen.

When I tell people this story, they're amazed that I worked through the tragedy. But I see those two months as just a blip on the radar. In fact, I'm sure I could have made a lot more sales during those two months if I wasn't in the hospital. I just knew I had to keep things moving along, working hard as ever, if I was going to reach my goal of being No. 1.

Of course, you have to know your limits. Through the years, our organization has become more vocal about promoting a balance. I expect my associates to work hard, but I can't require them to keep the same hours I keep. Of course, they have schedules to stick to, but I'm careful not to burn them out with excessive hours. Like a lot of entrepreneurs, I have to stay conscious of this because I'm such a workhorse so I don't burn out. So we promote the idea of working hard while you're here but maintaining a balance in your life around work.

"Rick is so passionate about the business and he's so focused on the business, so when you're at work, there wasn't much time for anything else but work," says former longtime career associate Bob Bartholomew. "That's one thing I admired about him. If you're involved in this business, you're going to be involved in it to the fullest. He was committed to it and he got people that worked with him committed to it, as well, and that's why he's been so successful.

"There were many times when we had advertising meetings at 5 in the morning. That's a high expectation, but on the other hand, Rick has always compensated his people well, provided for them, and made them as comfortable as possible, keeping in mind the pressures and the intensity of the cyclical automobile business. It's a high-pressure job, and he realizes that. He'll push people to the limits, but he knows when to back off."

It comes down to planning and prioritizing — that's how you optimize your workday. I always carry a Day-Timer personal calendar with me to stay very organized. First thing every morning, I make a schedule of all the calls I must make, meetings I must attend, and other tasks at hand. I prioritize with the most important ones on top in my Day-Timer. Then, the next morning, if there are any unfinished tasks, I move them to that day's priorities. That's how I make sure I stay on top of everything that needs to be done.

"The No. 1 thing I've learned from Rick Case is how to use a Day-Timer," says Jack "JJ" Jackintelle, the president and COO of the Rick Case Auto Group. "He literally spent two days teaching me how to be organized in my planning and in my organizational skills to efficiently manage 15 dealerships, 1,000 employees, customers, and future growth. To run a company this big, you can't wing it. This Day-Timer is something I'll have for the rest of my life because he was able to show me how to get extremely organized and stay ahead and not end up buried."

My associates know this Day-Timer is an extension of myself. They know that if I say, "OK, Bill, get back to me on Thursday," then I will write their name in my book under Thursday. That ensures follow-up, for me as well as for him. Follow-up is so crucial, and not just in terms of calling people back. Follow-up is how you get from an idea to execution. You can't just come up with an idea or set a goal. It's easy to sit around the conference table and say, "That sounds like a good idea," or, "Oh, let's do this." It takes commitment to say, "OK, then let's write this down. This is what needs to be done next. Let's get this done by this date."

By keeping track of every day, I can better visualize what I need to accomplish. Having things written down helps me focus on the task at hand. When I'm working on the first item on my to-do list, I'm 100 percent focused on No. 1 so I don't get distracted by No. 12. That's really my secret for staying so productive and balanced, because then when it's family time, I can switch my focus entirely to that.

When you're the first one in the office, working more hours than anyone else, you will get the best opportunities for the most business. But if you're the first one in the office and the last one to leave at the expense of your home life or your health or other priorities, are you really achieving success? It is those entrepreneurs who can learn to balance their schedules who rise to the top, make the most money, and go furthest in their careers.

SIX ☆ Tues., Jan. 27, 1970 Akron Beacon Journal B 1

BARBERTON FIREMAN George Culbertson battles flames which caused an estimated $100,000 in damages at Rick Case Honda Monday afternoon. Some 75 motorcycles, four automobiles and a major portion of the building were destroyed following an explosion caused by gasoline fumes ignited by a heater. Owner Rick Case underwent emergency surgery for second and third degree burns of the face, chest, arms and legs. He is "satisfactory" at Barberton Citizens Hospital. Others treated were employes Mrs. Dorothy Gandee and Thomas Heller and Barberton fireman James Hatula.

Article in the Akron Beacon Journal about the fire, 1970

Millionaire before 30th birthday

The TIMES-REPORTER D-3
Tues., July 2, 1974
DOVER-NEW PHILADELPHIA, OHIO

Rick Case: 'Boy wonder' of cycle world

He's called the "boy wonder" of the recreational vehicle field, but as Rick Case sees it, there's no magic in business success, just a great deal of planning and hard work.

One of his goals was to become a millionaire before age 30 and he accomplished that with time to spare. He set his sights on becoming the nation's largest motorcycle dealer and accomplished that well before his 30th birthday.

Now he's looking for new goals, and one has to do with his acquisition of the former Mathias Raceway, south of New Philadelphia. It has been re-named Rick Case Cycle Park and Case says, "I'd like to build it into the finest — and perhaps the biggest — motorcycle competition and recreation park in the country."

If his personal history repeats itself, that goal will be another check mark on his scoreboard in the near future.

Case entered the business world as a pre-teen. He started with a newspaper delivery route, but wasn't content to follow his single route day to day. He expanded, took on other routes and hired others to make the deliveries. In a short time his income exceeded that of any one of his delivery boys, "but I didn't have to go out in the rain to make deliveries."

BY THE time he reached his teens, Case was expanding into the automotive field. He started a used car reconditioning business before he was old enough to drive. "I had to hire older guys to shuttle the cars around," he said.

By the time he was a student at Kent State University, he owned the largest used car dealership in Summit County. A few years later, at age 23, he saw that expansion into another field was the only way to launch his own personal rocket.

He saw motorcycling as a star that was rising, analyzed the market potential and decided then was the time to move. Using the money from the sale of his used car business, he bought a Honda franchise and set up shop in Wooster.

From there, the climb has been steady, steep and calculated. Today his headquarters is a $1-million retail outlet in Cuyahoga Falls. He has another $1-million store in Cleveland, and has stores in Kent, Wooster, Barberton, East Cleveland and Parma Heights. He sells Honda, Yahama, Kawasaki and Suzuki motorcycles.

He recently expanded into the 10-speed bicycle market, and carries the full line of St. Etienne French racing bicycles at each of his eight stores.

In addition, Case has dealerships selling and servicing Toyota, Fiat and Honda cars, and he owns a wholesale distributing company.

Asked about the future of the transportation market, Case said, "It's bound to go up and up."

Since every vehicle he sells is considered a fuel economy machine, and looking at the current — almost frantic — upward trend in economy and vehicle sales, it looks as if yet another goal is about to be reached.

★ ★ ★

RICK CASE STANDS AMONG PART OF HIS MASSIVE MOTORCYCLE KINGDOM

Enthusiasm, hard work

Opening-at-a-glance

THURSDAY

Motocross — amateur and expert
Seven race series
Trophies and cash
Practice at 8:30 a.m., racing at noon
Movie: "On Any Sunday"
Fireworks display

FRIDAY

Night short-track
Gary Bailey Motocross School
Motocross action films
Movie: "On Any Sunday"
Free camping each night

SATURDAY

Night short-track
Gary Bailey Motocross School
Old-fashioned Beer Nite
FREE Barbequed Chicken & Pepsi
Movies and action films

SUNDAY

Motocross — amateur and expert
Practice at 8:30 a.m., racing at noon
Free AMA rule books to all competitors

Article in Times-Reporter, 1974

Rick Case in his first corporate and CEO offices in Cuyahoga Falls, Ohio, 1971

Rick honored as the "King of Kawasaki" in 1977 as the world's largest volume Kawasaki motorcycle dealer.

Chapter 4

Lesson #4: Capture the customer's attention

The first necessary ingredient for a successful business is the customer. Without customers, a business can't exist. Without satisfied customers, a business can't survive and thrive. Organizations that satisfy customers are always doing things that the customers want, things that make them feel good, and things that make the customer want to buy from them.

First, you need to capture the customer's attention. That takes advertising, and the most effective advertising is both frequent and creative. If your message is fresh and you get out in front of people frequently, it's going to stick. It wasn't uncommon for me to run 40 radio spots a week on one station during the '70s and '80s. And I was the first car dealer in the area to put a full-page ad in a newspaper. I budgeted $100,000 for a three-month television campaign to promote motorcycles, which was significant in the early 1970s.

As far as creative advertising, a lot of that just came naturally. But you can actually stretch creativity even further with your commitment. When you have a burning desire to sell everybody everything that you can — to be No. 1 — you spend a lot of your time thinking about new ways to make that happen. There was one commercial, for example, where I jumped off the roof of the dealership onto an airbag and, with some editing tricks, it looked like I slid right into an open sunroof. In the 1970s, that kind of TV ad was extremely unusual. There was not the same kind of technology as there is today, and you really had to perform the stunt to film it.

It was both the amount of advertising I did and the crazy one-of-a-kind ideas I came up with to do it that made me a household name around Cleveland. Rick Case became synonymous with Honda. My voice became recognizable because I was doing so much TV and radio advertising.

At first, I wasn't sure I wanted to go on air to do my own promotions. I was comfortable having John Lanigan do my commercials for me. He is a well-known voice around Cleveland as a morning drive radio host on oldies channel Majic 105.7.

"We encouraged him to do that," Lanigan says. "In the beginning, he didn't do that, and we kept saying, 'You've got to do this.' And then, 'This sounds really good,' the first time he tried it. After that, 'That's a keeper. You've got to keep doing that.' And it became a lot of fun. He liked doing commercials. It became iconic because that was Rick Case: 'Hi, I'm Rick Case.'"

Having strategically expanded into the four corners of the Cleveland market, what I really did was maximize my advertising reach. When you have multiple locations across the market, you can afford to spend more on advertising because you're serving more of the market. A dealer on the northeastern side of Cleveland might run a radio ad, and he's only getting 25 cents for every dollar because he's serving only a quarter of the market. From my position in Cleveland all the way down to Akron, I received a full return because of my market saturation. Once you spread out geographically, it makes advertising much more efficient.

When I opened my fourth dealership in Kent, for example, we held a weeklong grand-opening celebration. At each location, we had refreshments and gave away a free Honda motorcycle. I promoted the event like crazy using the best tools of the time. We advertised it in an eight-page tabloid newspaper supplement in the Akron Beacon Journal, which had a circulation of a quarter million readers back then. We also advertised on two local "Top 40" radio stations with a schedule of 200 60-second spots. It was a great success.

I have found those kinds of promotions, where you build an entire event around some occurrence, to be the best and most efficient way to keep your name in front of the public, and maximize traffic to the showroom. Once I realized this,

I began developing unique promotions, one after another. Nearly all my advertising, even to this day, is based on some sort of promotion. Done correctly, extensive promotions can hit customers through several different media, creating the greatest impact for the least expense.

In general, two types of promotions have worked well for me — the tie-in and the personal appearance. I work a lot with local media, as well as fellow retailers, to put on events and contests. This collaborative type of advertising often costs very little and can end up being very effective because you maximize your effort with the help of partners.

Because I was working with radio stations so often to advertise, it made sense to start working together on events and tie-in promotions, too. In 1966, I worked with some local TV guys to produce one of the first outdoor rock concerts in the country with multiple performers. I remember picking up Neil Diamond at the airport — he'd come in on a commercial flight — and driving him to the concert in my Jaguar XKE. We took over the entire park at Chippewa Lake Amusement Park in Medina County on Labor Day weekend: Sept. 1 – 4, 1966. The Ohio Teen Fair, we called it, happened on an outdoor state we built. This was still a couple of years before Woodstock, so we put on an outdoor rock concert before most people ever heard of them.

Promotions just come naturally to me. I was always promoting events that I thought would attract people. I started the process by asking one question: What would make the customer want to come to this and have a good time here? If that was the starting point, it would also be the result.

One of the first major events I put on in the 1960s was designed just to give people a good time. It wasn't focused on selling or philanthropy. Instead, Rick Case Appreciation Day was created to appreciate our customers.

Every summer, for this event, I would rent a racetrack —

Dragway 42, a drag strip in West Salem, Ohio — and invite everyone out so they could run their motorcycles up and down the drag strip or just watch others do it. They had to come into one of our dealerships and pick up the tickets. They didn't need to buy a car or a motorcycle from me or anything. Anybody who wanted to attend could. And so it became this big party all weekend long, with people camping out, bands performing, and people riding their motorcycles up and down the drag strip.

Customers loved Rick Case Appreciation Day. It became such a hit that thousands of people showed up for it each year. It grew so big that Hot Rod Magazine, the biggest car magazine in the country, sent a reporter out to write a story about this huge event in 1969.

One of the regular performers was Art Arfons, the world land speed record-holder. With his help, one year we featured the world's fastest toad — which sat in Arfons's lap as he drove his 17,500-horsepower jet down the quarter-mile track in 6.16 seconds. That toad probably set a record, going almost 255 miles per hour with Arfons. The customers really liked seeing Arfons, toad or no toad, racing down the drag strip in his jet cars.

Arfons was real familiar with my dealerships because he was a customer. Over the years, he made several appearances at my stores with his jet cars and dragsters. Not only would he draw large crowds of people to my showrooms, but he was also one of my best salesmen because he was a great Honda enthusiast who spoke highly of the brand every chance he had. That made it pretty easy to get him on board for events.

The next big celebrity I went after for this event was Evel Knievel. I called him and explained the success I'd had with my motorcycle dealerships and the Rick Case Appreciation Day, and I asked him if he would participate. He agreed to come to Appreciation Day and do a jump. As much as his appearance brought some bang to our event, it really helped him, too, because of all the press coverage I got him.

On May 28, 1974, Knievel jumped over 10 Mack trucks at the Rick Case Appreciation Day during the Memorial Day weekend. Earlier that same day, he drove the Indy 500 pace car and flew into my event by helicopter. That was his final jump in the United States until the Snake River Canyon jump in Idaho.

Knievel liked the way I promoted him at Rick Case Appreciation Day — so much that he asked me to help him with other events. I thought it would be fun to work with this crazy motorcycle jumper, so I started promoting in addition to running the motorcycle and car dealerships. I worked with Knievel in the summer of 1974 promoting the Snake River Canyon jump.

The Snake River Canyon happened on Sept. 8, 1974. Knievel hired an aeronautical engineer to build a rocket-powered cycle for the jump. It would have been wild watching this rocket-cycle hybrid fly across and land, but the parachute accidentally deployed and dragged him along the canyon wall to the bottom of the canyon.

When I had Knievel appear at the Soap Box Derby in Akron in 1975, the promoter from Kings Island Theme Park near Cincinnati was in the crowd. Jim Gruber realized that Knievel's audience looked a lot like his own. He was looking for something special to bring people to the theme park in October, after school started and family vacations stopped.

Gruber knew about my work and friendship with Evel Knievel, so he asked for my help to secure him for an event. After a failed attempt at jumping 13 buses at Wembley Stadium in England, Knievel came away with severe injuries and very publicly announced he was done with long jumps. That didn't stop me from calling him to get him to jump again. His sights had been set on San Francisco, but he knew that with my help as a promoter, a publicized jump in Ohio could bring him back.

Along with Gruber and Bill Price, who was the marketing director at Kings Island, I flew out to Butte, Montana, Knievel's hometown. He signed the contract, agreeing to jump at Kings Island, just in time to pre-tape an announcement that would air that evening right after ABC's documentary about him, called "Portrait of a Daredevil."

That began the countdown for us to set up the jump to Knievel's specifications. Kings Island had to build an arena with bleachers in the parking lot for spectators, and during construction, Knievel would fly over the site in a helicopter and name off the alterations he wanted, like widening the ramp. We all kept thinking it would be his last long jump, and that's why he was being so particular.

For the second year in a row, I spent the summer promoting another Evel Knievel jump. We did appearances for this jump in Cleveland, Akron, Columbus, Indianapolis, Louisville, and Cincinnati. While we were in Cincinnati, the two of us played golf with legendary comedian Bob Hope and Johnny Bench, the greatest baseball catcher of all time. I remember that game — Knievel yelling at me for driving the golf cart across the green, and Bob Hope's wife with their little white poodle. I'll never forget that.

The Kings Island jump was scheduled for Oct. 25, 1975, five months after Knievel's fall at Wembley. I was able to get Greyhound to bring in 14 buses for him to jump over. About 20,000 people bought dual tickets to the park that day, which included admission to the jump, and another 5,000 bought tickets for the jump alone. The entire hourlong motorcycle show, climaxing with Knievel's performance, was televised. The whole thing was a huge success. At 133 feet, it was the longest jump he completed in his career. And it achieved the highest viewer ratings in the history of ABC's Wide World of Sports, attracting 52 percent of the TV audience — or about 55 million people, which was more than the number of people that watched the Kentucky Derby. The Kings Island jump was the greatest success of Evel Knievel's career.

Another celebrity I went after to perform at Rick Case Appreciation Day was a motorcyclist from California named Russ Collins. He built a drag bike powered by three four-cylinder Honda engines, making it the fastest quarter-mile drag motorcycle in the world at that time. He came to Rick Case Appreciation Day in 1976 to drag race this freight train of a machine. It hit a speed of 170 miles an hour before he lost control and crashed. He ended up in the hospital in my hometown of Akron with a few broken ribs and fingers, some stitches, a collapsed lung, and a ruptured spleen and gall bladder. With a commitment and a desire like my own, Collins was busy designing his next bike before he left the hospital.

Because of the promoting I was doing for Evel Knievel, other performers started coming to me. So I started a company called Rick Case Productions to handle all of the entertainers I was promoting. There was Mr. Backwards, whose real name was Roger Riddell. He became known as the world's first and only motorcycle jumper who rode backwards. He once jumped seven cars — a whopping 60 feet — and earned a place in the Guinness Book of World Records. I booked him for several jumps, including one in the Houston Astrodome.

I promoted other record-breakers, like the McGuire twins, Billy and Benny, who held the Guinness Record for "World's Heaviest Twins" at about 800 pounds each. One of the famous pictures of them came from when I put them each on Honda mini-bikes — it was a pretty amusing scene. I also worked with A.J. Pagunas, who would jump off of buildings onto an airbag.

To succeed at the promotions business, I researched what successful promoters did to achieve successful events. Since I'd been involved with marketing and selling motorcycles and cars since 1962, a lot of this promotional work just came naturally. It didn't matter whether I was selling motorcycles or motorcyclists.

The key to all of it was remembering that no matter what I did, it was all about the customer. Part of this is ensuring the customer receives value from whatever it is you're doing, whether you're selling them a product or an experience. Value doesn't necessarily mean deal in terms of price; value also means getting customers to have fun, entertaining them, or letting them see and meet celebrities. Some of the best promotions I've done — like Rick Case Appreciation Day — were just about giving customers a good time. And they worked.

Rick Case, motorcycle man

By BRUNO BORNINO

"Last year we sold 10,000 motorcycles. This year we hope to triple that."

Impecably dressed in the latest double knit tan suit, wide tie, striped brown and yellow shirt and white boots, 29-year-old Rick Case looked the part of the most successful motorcycle dealer in the United States.

It was 8 a.m., and Case already had put in three hours of work at his million-dollar dealership in Cuyahoga Falls.

"I usually don't start until six," he said, "but there was a management meeting this morning, and I needed the extra hour to prepare for it."

Case doesn't have too many "extra hours". He generally works 18 hours a day, seven days a week at being "The Motorcycle Man."

"I don't look at it as work," he said between sips of coffee and answering a constantly ringing phone. I love motorcycles and everything connected with the business. To me it's all fun."

Whatever he chooses to call it — work or fun — selling motorcycles has been very profitable for Case.

He has seven other dealerships in the Cleveland-Akron area just like the one he uses as headquarters in Cuyahoga Falls. Through this multi-million-dollar chain he's responsible for about 70% of all motorcycle sales in this area.

Case employs 300, including 30 mechanics. His salesmen frequently sell 100 motorcycles in a single day.

Honda motorcycles are featured at five of the dealerships, and Kawasaki cycles at two others. Case has been the top Honda dealer in the U.S. three straight years, and is also the nation's No. 1 Kawasaki dealer.

"We opened our first Suzuki dealership at 6708 Pearl Rd., across from Southland Shopping Center in Parma Heights last week," he said. "It's a fine location, and initial response has been very encouraging."

Translated that means Case will probably be the nation's top Suzuki dealer soon.

"There are more than 12 million motorcycle riders in the U.S. today," he said. "It's easily the fastest-growing retail business.

"And this is only the beginning," he continued, adding that his business has increased by at least 300% each year since he stopped selling used cars and began selling motorcycles in 1966.

CHAIN REACTION — Operating from his Cuyahoga Falls office, Rick Case keeps in phone contact with officials from his seven other motorcycle stores. Case holds at least one four-hour meeting per week with his store managers.

(Press photo by Bill Nehez)

"I don't see any reason for that trend to change, because this is a youth-oriented business. More than 50% of the cycle owners are 25 or younger, and 75% of the mini-bike owners are between 10 and 16."

Case also owns Associated Distributing Co., which supplies all of his retail outlets with parts, accessories and supplies.

"Motorcycles cost anywhere from $200 to $2000," he said. "Helmets, which are required for all drivers, are another $20 or $30."

Displaying a cycle-clothing inventory of more than $250,000, he explained that a leather jacket costs about $60, matching slacks another $60. Boots go for $20 to $60.

Case's goal is to make "motorcycle" a household word, and to do so he has budgeted more than $500,000 for advertising in newspapers, radio and television.

"We have some customers who have eight bikes for a family of five. Mom, dad and the kids all ride. We want more of those families."

Case is greatful to all his Cleveland-Akron customers and will prove it with an Appreciation Day at West Salem's Dragway 42 on Father's Day, June 18.

Cyclists will have command of the track. In addition to seeing some top attractions, riders will be allowed to do their own things from 9 a.m. to 6:30 p.m. More than 20,000 are expected, with free tickets available at all Rick Case locations.

Article about Rick Case, 1972

Rick Case Appreciation Day poster, 1977

Rick Case at his Rick Case Cycle Park he operated in 1974

Evel Knievel (left) with Rick Case (right), 1974

Evel Knievel signing autographs for children at Rick Case's corporate office, 1974

Mr. Backwards making a jump in 1976

Rick Case of **Sharp Used Cars**

AUTO SAFETY COMMENTS ON *"Speed is a Two-Edged Sword"*

Most of the safety features, comfort, styling and dependability, built into today's cars be contributed to speed on the race track where professional drivers and top mechanics working with engineers have created so many innovations such as rear view mirror, 4 wheel brakes, high pressure lubricating systems, high compression engines, torsion bar supension, stabilizer bar, streamlining and many, many others that have helped bring our present production autombiles to their now high quality.

And the new model automobile today is a good machine capable of sustained turnpike speeds, and very good safety capability if properly driven. In plain words today's auto is much safer than today's average driver, because today's auto alone has made it possible for, non-professional, average, in-apt and even downright poor drivers to travel 60 miles an hour on turnpikes, expressways and non-congested areas in comparative safety.

At this point speed shows the other edge of its sword which can easily turn into a scythe of death. At speeds, in excess of 60 miles an hour the average non-professional driver is incapable of coping with a real emergency because he has never had the opportunity or training to put his car into slides, spins, tough braking positions, or trained his reactions to super speeds as a professional has been required to do. The best way to describe the effect of speed on traction, from 60 miles an hour and on up to 100 or more is that on a good dry road, in a slide caused by too quick a turn or in braking quickly the reaction will be the same as a moist surface at 70 on up to plain ice at 100 plus m.p.h.

Overconfidence should be avoided above all by the non-professional driver so he will not exceed his speed capabilities, this definitely includes the traffic light drag star who has learned to shift through the gears like lightning. Under present day availability and training he never really gets a chance to find out if he can truly handle the car until he is in a position where all the chips are down, and when more likely than not he can not handle the situation. Speed the grim reaper, wins again.

So hold safe speed and enjoy the many happy hours and miles the auto holds in store for you.

RICK CASE,
SHARP USED CARS
353 Wooster Rd.
Phone 753-2261

Rick promoting his Sharp Used Car Lot at the Ohio Teen Fair, 1966

Chapter 5

Lesson #5: Build confidence in your product

If you don't have confidence in your product, you'll never convince the customer to have confidence in it. Even the best salesman must believe in the product he is selling before he'll have success.

Honda's first car sold for $1,635 MSRP. With its two-cylinder 600cc air-cooled engine, it was a joke at the time in the industry. Even when they rolled out the Civic in 1973, which was a much better-made, four-cylinder car that sold for $2,150, people still didn't have much confidence in the brand. Other dealers were even telling buyers, "It's a car with a motorcycle engine," and, "You don't want that dinky little thing."

My challenge, then, was to convince U.S. consumers that they should try a new car they'd never heard of while others poked fun at it.

The solution was to find a way to either reduce or eliminate their risk. I recognized that I needed to make people feel confident about buying a Honda. That started with showing them how confident I was in the car.

There really were a lot of positive things to say about the Honda car. Honda had a great name as a motorcycle then, so it was easy to talk about Honda reliability and price. I had driven the car, so I had faith that it would stand up against the competing import and domestic brands that people were more familiar with. So I figured, why not give prospective buyers the opportunity to draw the same conclusion? That's how I came up with the idea to design my "Dare to Compare" marketing strategy, where I would have new competitor brands at the dealership for customers to test drive. I bought a Ford Falcon, a Volkswagen Beetle, a Chevy Vega, a Toyota Corolla, and a

Datsun 210 — which is now part of the Nissan brand — and put them all on my Honda lot.

In my advertising, I would say, "We have a new Ford, Chevy, VW, Toyota, and Datsun here for you to drive and compare to Honda so you can see why Honda is the best."

Nobody had ever heard of doing that. The other dealers would not take the risk of having the competition on the lot. This method of introducing a new franchise into the market worked. It brought in a lot of people to see what the Honda Civic was all about. In fact, that marketing was key to our sales success in the early Honda introduction and made us the largest Honda car dealer in America.

Beyond that, to further reduce — if not completely eliminate — the risk of buying a Honda, I offered a 10-day free trial money-back guarantee that allowed customers to return the car if it didn't exceed all of their expectations. The advertising said, "Buy a Honda, and if you're not completely satisfied for any reason, bring the car back within 10 days or 500 miles and we'll give you your money back."

Dealers thought I was crazy to offer a free trial. They couldn't believe a dealer would actually do something like that. When they looked at that promotion, all they saw was risk. That was just so far out of the box.

Then, in 1973 and '74, the Middle East oil embargo pushed gas prices up above 30 cents a gallon. When the gas crisis hit, a lot of dealers viewed it as a negative. I didn't. Instead, I saw opportunity and used the problem to help me conceive new ways to promote and sell my cars. With consumers starting to worry about rising gas prices, they would start looking more closely at fuel-efficient options, like the vehicles I carried.

I lined up truckloads of Civics along the street in front of my dealership. I owned a gas station next door to the dealership, where gas was up to about 30 cents a gallon. There were huge lines at gas stations everywhere because the embargo on gasoline created rationing. And I wanted to share in the attention gas stations garnered.

I changed the price on my gas station's sign so that it read 99 cents a gallon. I would have gone higher, but at that time, no one thought gas would ever be more than a dollar so the signs only had room for two numbers. I had a newspaper photographer come out and take pictures that ended up on the front page of the newspaper. They showed all of these truckloads of Honda cars lined up and the price of gas at 99 cents at a time when it was only about 30 cents. People wondered if Rick Case had the foresight. What if gas prices keep going up? Which car will give me the best value then? Well, this new Civic, of course.

The Civic offered a lot of value for the money. Between 1973 and '74, in the midst of this gas embargo, national Civic sales increased sevenfold. Then sales quadrupled from '74 to '76. Honda's relentless focus on quality and efficiency was very desirable in a marketplace where a lot of American cars had big engines and poor fuel economy compared to Honda.

All in all, I had lots of reasons to tout Hondas as a good buy when customers were pinched at the pump. Still, I went another step further and guaranteed gas mileage at 30 miles per gallon for the Honda Civic. In those days, the average car got between 8 and 10 miles per gallon. I told people that if they didn't get 30 miles per gallon, they could return the car within 30 to 60 days or 600 to 3,000 miles and I'd buy their car back. This was just another way to reduce the risk of buying a Honda.

I always did promotions that addressed customers' concerns, such as the rising gas prices. People were concerned about filling their tanks. Some dealers saw that as a challenge, but I saw it as an opportunity to build promotions right into the crisis. It takes a lot of creativity to benefit from forces you can't control. But when your customers are worried about those things, you have to be able to present your product in a way that makes them feel like the problem is solved.

Those promotions can be a lot of fun. One successful promotion that sprung from the rising gas prices was pretty simple. The idea was: How far can a Honda go on just two gallons of gas?

To accomplish this, I secured the six top radio personalities from Cleveland's radio stations and the No. 1 weatherman from TV and put them each in a Honda Civic 1500 five-speed. Each car started with exactly two gallons of gasoline. For two months beforehand, people would write in to guess how far the Honda car would go and which local celebrity would go the furthest. We received more than 25,000 entries.

The celebrities started at our dealership in Cleveland and headed down I-71 toward Columbus. We selected that direction to promote Honda's new manufacturing plant located in Marysville, just north of Columbus — the first Japanese car plant in America.

The trophy went to Dick Goddard, who's still a TV weatherman in Cleveland. He wanted to have his lucky black cat with him in his car during the drive, which I remember was pretty funny and garnered him some extra attention. He ended up logging 87.7 miles.

The real winner, though, was Wyatt Lewis from North Canton, who wrote in and guessed the best combination of celebrity and how far he drove. The lucky guesser received the choice between a new 1981 Honda or a used 1956 Rolls Royce Silver Cloud. That got us a lot of coverage in the newspapers, on TV, and on the radio. Comparing a Rolls Royce, the most expensive and luxurious car in the country — in the world, at that time — to this little Honda was such an extreme promotion. The winner did not choose the Rolls as the prize, that's for sure. Four of the radio DJs even decided to buy the Hondas they drove in the contest afterward.

Some of my other promotions seemed just as extreme simply because nobody else had thought of them before. In the 1970s, I began offering roadside service, for example. The press really buzzed about this promotion. Typically, the radio and TV spots went something like this: "If you buy a car from me and you run out of gas, I'll bring you gas. If you break down, I'll come out and tow you in. If you get a flat tire, I'll come change it — 24 hours a day, seven days a week, anywhere in the country."

It was a great promotion because it was like I was saying, "I'm personally going to do this for you." Dealers couldn't figure out how I could make these claims. They wondered how I could deliver gas to someone anywhere in the country. People would come up to me at restaurants to say, "How do you do that? Aren't you too busy to be here if you're changing tires across the country?"

Nobody could figure it out, but it was actually really simple. All I did was go to AAA and make a deal. For every car I sold, I would buy the owner a membership to AAA. At the time, the cost was about $12 per car, per year. So AAA was my agent, so to speak, who was responsible for changing tires, towing cars, and providing gasoline. But because I was the one providing the service for my customers, I could make the claim that I'd cover the copied my idea and provided roadside assistance.

What's fascinating, in retrospect, is that the combination of all these offers — which all really just reduced the buyer's risk — was what made us so successful. When an entrepreneur can keep devising new, creative ways to make buyers feel more confident about their purchasing decisions, you will maximize your sales.

In 1972, '73, and '74, our stores consistently ranked in the top three spots nationally for Honda in terms of sales volume. It was all because I understood the power of building consumer confidence in my product.

Rick in the first Honda car sold in the U.S. (at the Honda museum Calif. 2011) The first Honda model sold, a 1970 N600

Truck loads of Honda Civics in front of the Cuyahoga Falls dealership, 1973

Rick Case (right) with Soichiro Honda (left) at Rick's Cleveland Honda dealership, the largest Honda motorcycle dealership and largest Honda sign in the U.S., 1973

Chapter 6

Lesson #6: Two heads are better than one

A lot of CEOs face a dilemma when they realize there are few people to turn to for guidance: It can be lonely at the top. This lesson hit many new Honda dealers because there was little education available for introducing this brand to the country — especially not for those rare few, like myself, who came to it by way of motorcycles.

Dealers in other franchises had connected through the National Automobile Dealers Association and had set up NADA 20 Groups, made up of 20 dealers of the same brand from non-competing markets at least 500 miles apart. A few of us were trying to get the same group going for Honda dealers so we could get together to share ideas, share sales data, and improve business growth.

The main force behind the creation of that first Honda NADA 20 Group was a young woman from California who'd grown up in a Honda car/motorcycle dealership: Rita Manly. Her parents opened a Honda motorcycle dealership in Santa Rosa in 1959. Then, in 1968, they were awarded the very first Honda car franchise in the country, and they became the first to sell the brand's first U.S. car, the N600, in 1970.

Rita started out putting parts away and cleaning motorcycles, then later answering phones and finishing paperwork in the dealership office. Then, during high school, Rita sold cars and motorcycles. After she graduated from college, she became general manager of Honda of Santa Rosa. She was passionate about her parents' dealership and had the goal to become a successful car dealer.

At the second Honda NADA 20 group meeting in Hawaii in 1978, Rita was the only one in the group who could match my passion for selling — and selling Hondas in particular. The two of us pretty much dominated the group. And because we were the only two singles there, it didn't take long for us to develop an exclusive NADA 2 Group of our own on the side. While the other dealers did leisure activities we talked about how to improve our Honda car sales and our burning desire to be No. 1.

The NADA 20 Groups were designed as idea pools for dealers to share best practices from every facet of the business — in sales, service, and parts. We tossed around ideas about motivating employees, running better service departments, advertising, and marketing, compensating employees, and, of course, selling cars.

You can never think you know it all or you don't need help becoming more successful. These 20 Group meetings were an opportunity to bounce around ideas and learn from my peers. You're always learning. You can always be better.

"That's part of the reason why Rick has been so successful," Bob Bartholomew says. "He's always trying to learn from others. He always participated in these 20 Groups, coming back with ideas to try."

And you need to always be willing to help others, too. It's a give and take. As much as I learned from those meetings, I contributed back into them with ideas that had proven successful at Rick Case. At every meeting, three times a year, the group would hold a contest for the best idea. I won many of those because I brought such innovative marketing ideas to every meeting.

Meanwhile, Rita and I struck a special balance of that give and take of sharing ideas. Our relationship continued to grow as we traded ideas each week on the phone. She'd tell me what she wanted to do in parts and service, and I'd tell her my promotions for sales. We'd run ideas by one another before we rolled anything out at our dealerships.

We visited each other's dealerships, and we even held our own contests where we competed to beat each other as the best dealer in every area of the business.

After one of my best selling jobs ever, I asked Rita to marry me in 1979 and move from California to Akron, Ohio.

"The biggest thing I remember about the wedding was it was a snowy, cold, February night in Akron, Ohio," recalls Bartholomew, who attended our wedding. "He took Rita outside at the reception and there was a beautiful new red Ferrari sitting out there against that white snow background. That was his wedding present to her."

Rita and I joined forces — in life and in business — and began building an automotive group together with the mutual goal of becoming the No. 1 volume dealer for all of our brands with the highest customer satisfaction in the nation.

Rita became the fixed operations director for the group, which means she led the parts and service departments. Soon after, she added CFO to her responsibilities. Finance is one of her strongest assets. She received a Bachelor of Science degree in Economics from the University of California, and it was she who developed the first Honda franchise financial statement. Before then, Honda let its dealers submit financials on whatever forms they used for their other franchises. That meant there was no way to develop comparative data for the dealers to measure their performance or set benchmarks. Along with NADA, Rita initiated the development of the first standardized Honda financial statement that was approved by Honda, NADA, and Reynolds and Reynolds — a forms printer that provides standardized accounting forms for auto dealers.

Our division of duties works this way: I've always handled the marketing, factory relations, merchandising, inventory acquisition, and sales. Rita takes care of parts and service, finance, and personnel. By separating our workloads this way, we free each other up to focus on our individual strengths.

"I've never seen anything like the partnership Rick has with Rita," says Mike Jackson, chairman and CEO of AutoNation. "I've never seen anything like it in the business where they have complementary talents and abilities that make each other better in the business."

We are equally visible, inside the company and out. Most people recognize us from our TV commercials, promoting our dealerships. In all of the commercials, you'll always see Rita wearing her token accessory: a hat.

One of the things that has made it possible for us to achieve the remarkable success we've had in growing our business is that we're in the business together. The two of us are business partners in the truest sense of the word. We are able to maintain a balance because we share the same passion.

Most entrepreneurs have to deal with trying to balance their home life with their business goals, but not me. The conversations between Rita and me don't change from the office to the dinner table, like they do for 99.9 percent of entrepreneurs out there. Other entrepreneurs go home for dinner and the conversations become, "What did Susie do at school today?" But Rita and I talk business from the second we wake up until we lie back down to go to sleep.

For most people, that might seem like an unbalanced life. But for us, that is balance. By marrying another car dealer, I achieved the work/life balance that some entrepreneurs search for their whole lives. We have created a partnership where we continue to challenge each other to devise creative ways to improve the company and break our own records. It is an amazing marriage.

"I've never seen a couple play off each other as well as those two do," says Kerry Becker, of the Boys & Girls Clubs, who got to know us both through our charity work. "They can finish each other's sentences. They don't necessarily always agree, but they're open to each other's suggestions. It's really cool to see them. They are truly a team in everything they do."

Rita brought a lot of key skills to the company that complement my own. At the time, I had three Fiat, one Lancia, and two Honda auto dealerships, and several motorcycle dealerships in Ohio. It was a relatively small company. She was able to provide a foundation for growth by developing financial and managerial procedures to successfully run dealerships on a larger scale.

"It's a perfect combination," Bartholomew says. "Quite frankly, Rita has got to be — if not the sharpest female in the automobile industry — at least in the top three. She's incredibly intelligent about the business. She knows it inside and out. They just make a very dynamic duo when it comes to the business and their charity work. They are just two of a kind."

Rita is the foundation for my ideas. She ensures that the company will be able to meet any challenges I put to it.

"Rick is a marketing genius. He's a tremendously creative visionary who never knew there was a box to think out of," Rita says. "I tell him if I think his ideas can work logistically."

Of course, she comes up with some pretty good ideas of her own, too. While I focused on selling, marketing, and advertising, she concentrated on expanding maintenance and repair service at a time when most dealerships were only interested in doing warranty-related work. She started opening our service departments on Saturdays, which was very innovative at the time.

"I knew that if people came to Rick Case for service, we'd have a better chance of selling them a new car or motorcycle when they were ready," Rita says. "If you make it convenient for your customers, fix it right, and the pricing is fair, they'll come back."

That's why we get along so well — we both share a focus on our customers and what will make them happy. Sure, we're both passionate about being No. 1, but it's the unique way we run our business together that makes it so special.

So it's true in business as in life: Two heads are better than one. I was fortunate enough to find a business partner and wife in one, but the general lesson is that you can't do everything alone. Even the best entrepreneurs have both strengths and weaknesses, and if you only rely on your ideas, you may be missing something. If you really want to push yourself further and be really successful, you will have to reach out.

In my years as a business leader, I have learned the value of finding people you can learn from, bounce ideas around with, inspire, and be inspired by. I strive to pass that on to my associates by helping them push their ideas further.

Some of my old associates from the early days in Ohio remember how often I used to listen to motivational and leadership development tapes. When I would travel, often accompanied by colleagues, I'd toss one of those tapes in the car and we would listen to it on our way to our destination. Even a car ride is an opportunity to gain some inspiration and insight from someone else.

Page 6 American Honda Motor Co., Inc. October 1980

"I Do, I Do"

Some dealers will do anything to try to get more Hondas -- they'll even get married.

That's right. This past year has witnessed the first marriage between two Honda dealers. The bride wore a lovely tiered lace gown and the groom was attired in top hat and tails as Rita Manly and Rick Case were wed recently in Akron, Ohio.

Rita Manly virtually grew up in the Honda business. In 1960, her parents, Bill and Lori, opened a Honda motorcycle shop, and their automobile dealership in Santa Rosa, California, was the first franchise signed with American Honda Motor Company.

A graduate of the University of California at Davis, Rita worked at her parents dealership, with the goal of becoming General Manager. She attained that goal and joined the first Honda NADA 20 group when it was forming. It was there that she first met Rick Case.

From a used car dealer at age 16, Rick has become one of the largest Honda automobile dealers in the country. He began his first Honda motorcycle shop in 1966 and now has two automobile dealerships, one in Cleveland and one in Akron, Ohio, and six multiple line motorcycle stores.

Their common interest in Honda automobiles and the improvement of their operations led them to the Honda NADA 20 group as well as to each other.

Now, Rita and Rick are working together for Honda from Rick Case Enterprises in Cuyahoga Falls, Ohio, and Rita's brother, Brian, manages Honda of Santa Rosa.

This true life love story gives credence to a fact we were always sure of: "You meet the nicest people at Honda."

Married in Akron, Rita and Rick now work together for Honda.

A Piece of Cake . . .

Ms. Pat Brown was so pleased with her new Accord and Mancuso Honda's support personnel, that she decided to express her appreciation in a very visible way.

So, recently, she went to the Barrington, Illinois, dealership and presented Salesman, Earl Getlin, and Service Advisor, Mark Rovnyak, with a huge "Thank You" cake.

Robert Mancuso, Owner, felt the gift was most appropriate because selling Honda's has always been "a piece of cake!"

Salesman, Earl Getlin, and Service Advisor, Mark Rovnyak, happily accept a "Thank You" cake from Ms. Pat Brown.

"Jimmy & Rose" Update

For any of you who saw and enjoyed Matar Honda's "Jimmy & Rose" advertising strip, which appeared in the April issue of *Honda Views*, we have good news.

Owner, Sam Matar, has copyrighted the strip and is now contracting with interested dealers to produce individualized strips for their facilities.

If you'd like a personalized strip for your dealership, contact Sam Matar, Matar Honda, Dealer 6940, (408) 899-3713.

Rita and Rick Case's wedding featured in the Honda monthly newsletter, first two Honda dealers to marry, 1980

Rita and Rick Case, 1981

Rita and Rick share a passion for Honda motorcycles, in their Honda Powerhouse Showroom, 2009

Rita and Rita Case in a Carrera

Rita and Rick on a Honda 50cc at the Honda museum in Calif. (2011) The first Honda motorcycle sold in the U.S. in 1959. Honda's tag line "You meet the nicest people on a Honda"

Rita and Rick visiting the Honda automobile manufacturing plant in Alabama while touring across country, 2005

Chapter 7

Lesson #7: Treat every customer as you would your best friend

The future of the Rick Case Auto Group rides heavily on two words: customer relations. The best way to build good customer relations is to treat every customer as you would your best friend.

This was one of the first lessons I learned in my early days of business, and it has become our company's core motto. In fact, this motto has even become our customer service training method.

I describe it to our associates like this: "If your best friend was coming in to buy or service a car today, you would do things a lot differently."

When associates think about that — whether they're in sales, service, or parts — and begin to see every customer as a friend, they give them more attention. What makes this kind of relationship-based selling so effective is that it's flexible. You don't have to memorize specific responses to certain input; you only need to remember that one rule: Treat the customer as you would your best friend. When you do, it's a win-win for both sides.

Success depends on ensuring that customers are happy from the time you greet them to the moment you hand them the keys to their new car. To accomplish this, you must understand where customers are coming from and what they want, starting with how they see your industry.

You have to be aware of where you stand, because the industry standard is the benchmark you're trying to transcend. Our sales training, for example, starts with a TLC exercise to get associates to "Think Like a Customer" by brainstorming how consumers see the automotive industry, dealers, and car salesperson, specifically.

Most customers look forward to going to a car dealership like patients look forward to a trip to the dentist, but it's because those customers haven't had a good experience at other dealerships. You overcome this by exceeding the customer's expectations so you can gain his or her respect immediately. And when customers don't expect much from your industry, you can easily impress them with the most common courtesies.

Here's an example. When customers walk into a Rick Case dealership, a manager greets them with, "Welcome to Rick Case. My name is John Smith, I'm the sales manager here. Here's my business card. Please note my home and cell number are included because at Rick Case, we're available to serve our customers 24 hours a day. By the way, here's Mr. Case's card, too, with his home phone and cell phone. In a moment, you'll be speaking with one of our sales consultants, but I want you to know: If there's anything I can do for you at any time, I am just a phone call away."

Customers can't believe it. If you're one of those people who associate car dealerships with dentists, imagine walking into a Rick Case dealership where the manager greets you with his personal numbers, then says, "You can also call the owner. Here are his home and cell numbers." That kind of unlimited accessibility takes the edge off. You're left thinking, "Man, I've landed in the right place. I actually matter to these people." There's nothing like a great first impression.

After we've already exceeded your expectations, the next thing the manager says to you is, "All right, I'm going to take care of you. Let me introduce you to one of my best sales consultants."

That sales consultant then offers a similar greeting and hands you his card with his home and cell phone number on it. This continues with every person you meet: managers, sales associates, service advisors. We ask every one of our associates who comes in contact with a customer to have their home and cell phone numbers printed on their business cards. Think about it — if your best friends needed anything, you'd want them to be able to reach you.

Some people call, but most people don't. They respect your privacy. But if they really have an issue, they will call a manager. And if they can't get a manager, they'll call me.

I get four or five calls each week. I get a mixture of good calls, telling me what a great experience a person had, and other calls when someone has an issue that needs attention. It might be somebody whose car is taking a while to get done in the collision center, or it could be someone who feels they're not getting the right information.

On the weekends, when I'm in a dealership greeting customers, I'll get calls saying, "I'm in one of your dealerships and can't get the deal I thought I should. What can you do for me?" And then I'll have guys call me from a bar, passing the phone around, then they'll ask, "Is this really Rick Case?" and then burst into laughter.

Handing out your numbers really gives customers — all customers — a direct line, and that's the point. When customers have direct access to the owner, it also reminds associates to treat every customer as they would their best friend because they all know that any customer can go straight to Rick Case. That keeps them on their toes. If you think that helps them go out of their way to take care of their customers like a friend, you better believe it, because they don't want any of their customers calling Rick Case and complaining about anything.

The buck stops with me, because I can solve a problem on the phone in five minutes that might otherwise mushroom over a two-week period of time while my managers are figuring out what to do with it. The idea is to identify the problem and get it solved immediately instead of letting it go and letting customers talk to 10 people and tell them what a problem it was. Everyone knows I'm the end of the line, and when I say "no," they will take that for an answer because there's nowhere else to go.

Most other dealers won't take the time to take calls like that. These calls can be time consuming, and the dealers may be too busy working on other parts of their business that they feel are more important than a single customer issue. I feel you'd better learn how to make time for your customers because if you don't, they won't make the time for you. After all, there's nothing more important than the customer.

Associates are required to make time for customers, as well, even if they're not working directly with that customer. We have what we call the 10-Foot Rule: Any time an associate walks within 10 feet of a customer in our dealerships, the associate has to say, "Hi, thanks for being at Rick Case," or, "Thanks for shopping with us today." At most stores, associates run by customers instead of stopping to say hello. We would acknowledge our best friend if they were visiting, and that's why we do it.

Another rule is that if a customer asks for directions, whether it's to the service department or the restroom, just pointing in that direction isn't polite. Associates must walk the customer within three feet of the door or counter of the destination. If it were your best friend asking where to go, you'd say, "Sure, follow me. I'll introduce you to the service manager when we get there."

When you only have a couple of minutes to make a good first impression and start building a solid relationship, a few words can make a world of difference. That's why I'm particular about a few phrases you should not hear in our dealerships.

If the customer is standing alone, associates will not say,

"Can I help you?" When you ask that, customers will just shake their heads or say, "No thanks. I'm just looking." Helping customers is not an option at our dealerships, so associates will say, "Thanks for being at Rick Case. My name is Joe Jones. What's yours?"

And if the customer says, "Thank you," our associates are asked not to respond with, "No problem." That's the second forbidden phrase. If you say, "Thank you" to an employee at a Ritz-Carlton or a Four Seasons Hotel, they're going to say, "My pleasure," not, "No problem." It's negative in nature, and it's never a problem to help the customer — it's our business and our pleasure.

Even though this is a fairly simple approach, this best friend treatment isn't very common at car dealerships or many service companies. That's because everything we do, we do it for the customer, while many dealers only do it for their business. One big problem with most domestic carmakers was that they worked for the shareholders. They didn't work for customers to provide a great product and a great deal because they were more focused on shareholders' profit. Under this scenario, the customer came second.

When your first priority is the customer, your shareholders make money. The Japanese and Koreans understood that. They've always been making cars that customers want. General Motors and Chrysler had to go bankrupt before they figured out that the whole retail business is all about the customer. You've got to have those priorities straight if you want to succeed. The best part is that when you do what's good for the customer, your business ends up benefiting.

Unlike a lot of other dealers, I'm really not in the business of selling cars. I'm in the business of building relationships. And I remind our associates of this all the time. When you build relationships, you don't just sell one car. You'll end up selling many cars — and not just to them but also their families, friends, neighbors, and business associates.

Relationship marketing really works. When you combine that relationship building and best friend treatment with our guarantees, warranties, and customer benefits, like free car washes for life, the customer can see we're really different because we care. We do things to wow customers that other dealers dare not do because they think it's too risky and too expensive.

One of our biggest leaps in customer service came in March 2002. Essentially borrowing from the airlines' concept of frequent-flyer miles, we launched the Rick Case Rewards Card program nationally at all of our dealerships. Every customer who buys a vehicle from us gets his or her own card, embossed with his or her name and account number. Every time customers buy something from us — parts, services, new or used cars, or motorcycles — they accumulate points on their Rewards Card. For example, a new car earns 100,000 points, and a referral is worth 50,000 points. They can redeem those points for discounts on future purchases of services, parts, and vehicles. The card operates the free car wash at our dealerships, whether they're driving a car they bought from us or not.

Another way customers can use their Rick Case Rewards Card — and hundreds do every day — is to purchase discount gas at our gas station. When gas prices started spiking to record highs in 2004, I installed an eight-pump discount gas center at our biggest dealership, the Honda store in South Florida. We buy gas every day from the refinery at the seaport and pay the lowest price and sell it to our customers at that wholesale price. That means our customers pay anywhere from 5 to 30 cents less per gallon for our gas than they would anywhere else.

And it's not just for customers; it's for the community. When hurricanes hit Florida, we use our generator and invite emergency vehicles, doctors, and nurses to come fill up at our pumps when they can't get gas anywhere else. After they get the gas they need to perform their jobs, we open up the pumps for our customers. During the last big hurricane, CNN showed an aerial view of our dealership with 300 cars lined up to get gas.

My method for coming up with many of these benefits for customers is always asking myself this question: Why would a customer leave and not buy?

If customers want to test drive a competitor's car, they shouldn't have to leave to do it. So let's save them the trip and have the competition's cars at our dealerships to drive and compare to our brands. If they think they'll find a better warranty with another franchise, we let them know that we double all the factory warranties to provide the best coverage they'll find anywhere. To be successful in business, you have to think of reasons why people would leave without buying, and then create solutions for those obstacles.

CARS • TRUCKS • VANS • SUVs
MOTORCYCLES • SCOOTERS • GENERATORS
CERTIFIED PRE-OWNED VEHICLES & MORE!

RICK CASE FIAT
I-75 between GRIFFIN & ROYAL PALM • Davie/Weston
SALES: Mon-Sat 9-9 • Sun 11-5
SERVICE: Mon-Fri 9-6 • Sat 9-5
954.903.5311 | rickcasefiatusa.com

RICK CASE HONDA
I-75 at Griffin • Davie/Weston
SALES: Mon-Sat 9-9 • Sun 11-7
SERVICE: Mon-Fri 7-7 • Sat 7:30-4
EXPRESS SERVICE: Mon-Fri 7-7 • Sat 7:30-6 • Sun 11-5
COLLISION CENTER: Mon-Fri 7:30-6 • Sat 8-12
954.364.3000 | rickcasehonda.com

RICK CASE HONDA Cycles
I-75 at GRIFFIN • Davie/Weston
SALES & PARTS/ACCESSORIES: Mon-Sat 9-7 • Sun 11-7
SERVICE: Mon-Fri 8:30-7 • Sat 8:30-6
954.364.3201 | rickcasehonda.net

RICK CASE HYUNDAI
I-75 between GRIFFIN & ROYAL PALM • Davie/Weston
SALES: Mon-Sat 9-9 • Sun 11-7
SERVICE: Mon-Fri 7:30-6 • Sat 8-4
EXPRESS SERVICE: Mon-Fri 7:30-6 • Sat 8-4 • Sun 11-5
COLLISION CENTER: Mon-Fri 8-5:30
954.377.4100 | rickcase.com

RICK CASE ACURA
ON 441 at SUNRISE BLVD • Fort Lauderdale
SALES: Mon-Fri 9-9 • Sat 9-6 • Sun 12-5
SERVICE: Mon-Fri 7:30-6 • Sat 8-5
EXPRESS SERVICE: Mon-Fri 7:30-6 • Sat 8-5
954.587.1111 | rickcaseacura.com

RICK CASE HYUNDAI
ON 441 at SUNRISE BLVD • Fort Lauderdale
SALES: Mon-Fri 9-9 • Sat 9-6 • Sun 12-5
SERVICE: Mon-Fri 7:30-6 • Sat 8-5
EXPRESS SERVICE: Mon-Fri 7:30-6 • Sat 8-5
954.581.5885 | rickcase.com

"Rick Case Advantages" customer brochure

Rick Case
REWARDS PROGRAM

SAVE $100s, EVEN $1000s
Save 10% on Service, Parts & Accessories with earned Rewards Points!

Earn Rewards Points with every purchase in Sales, Service, Parts & Accessories. Redeem toward future purchases of new and used cars, vans, trucks, SUVs, motorcycles, scooters, ATVs, home generators, service, parts and accessories.

RICK CASE "Makes it Easy" TO REWARD YOURSELF!
Here's how it works.

PRODUCT PURCHASED	EARNED POINTS
New or Used Car/Truck/Van or SUV	100,000
Motorcycle, ATV, & Scooters	50,000
Home Generators	20,000
Family & Friends Referrals	50,000
Service, Parts & Accessory Purchases	500 per $10 purchase

No Annual Fee,...It's Free!

Valid for retail customers only. Points are not redeemable for cash. Points expire 5 years from date of issue. Please present your card to the cashier at each visit to receive your rewards points discount. Example: Receive 500 Rewards Points for every $10 purchased in service, parts & accessories. Example: 1,000 Rewards Points equal $1.00 in merchandise redemption value. Redeem earned points for up to 10% off in Service, Parts & Accessories, and up to 5% off in Sales. Program subject to change without notice.

Exclusively at Rick Case at No Additional Cost to you!

ONE STOP SHOPPING!
Toyota • Nissan • Hyundai • Honda
All at Rick Case for you to
DRIVE & COMPARE!

3 DAY FREE TRIAL
MONEY BACK GUARANTEE
If you are not completely satisfied simply return the vehicle within 3 days or 300 miles and we will give you a complete refund.

- HYUNDAI -
DOUBLE FACTORY WARRANTY
20 YEAR/200,000 MILE NATIONWIDE WARRANTY
WITH EVERY NEW HYUNDAI PURCHASE

TRADE-IN GUARANTEE
RICK CASE GUARANTEES THE HIGHEST PRICE FOR YOUR TRADE-IN WITH THE HYUNDAI ASSURANCE TRADE-IN VALUE GUARANTEE PROGRAM!
SEE INSIDE FOR MORE INFORMATION.

- HONDA/ACURA -
RICK CASE INCREASES THE FACTORY WARRANTY TO A
10 YEAR/100,000 MILE NATIONWIDE WARRANTY
WITH EVERY NEW HONDA/ACURA PURCHASE

Plus with your Rick Case Rewards Card
FREE CAR WASHES
for LIFE & DISCOUNT GAS

Rick Case
954-377-7400 Office
954-587-7916 Fax
954-234-1022 Cell
954-785-9071 Home
954-946-1128 Home Fax
rickcase@rickcase.com

AUTOMOTIVE GROUP
50TH ANNIVERSARY
1962-2012

875 North State Road 7 • Fort Lauderdale, FL 33317 • rickcase.com
SOUTH FLORIDA • ATLANTA • CLEVELAND
ACURA HYUNDAI HONDA CARS & CYCLES
MITSUBISHI KIA mazda Audi smart

Rick Case's business card

RICK CASE REWARDS CLUB
HYUNDAI HONDA ACURA
MITSUBISHI HONDA Audi
mazda smart
1234
RICK CASE

Rick Case's Rewards Card

The Discount Gas Center for Rick Case Rewards Card holders

Rita and Rick receive the J.D. Power and Associates Customer Satisfaction Award for Ohio and Florida from J. David Power, 1998

Years of J.D. Power and Associates customer satisfaction awards for outstanding customer service

Chapter 8

Lesson #8: Get people to like you

You hear it all the time: People buy from people they like.

That couldn't be truer. In surveys of customers, the No. 1 reason why people say they decided to buy a car is: "I liked the salesperson."

In the early years, we had invited customer focus groups to share more about their buying habits. These groups were made of five customers who bought cars from us and five others who came into the store but didn't buy. We can spend a lot of money advertising, promoting, and building big, beautiful dealerships, and the factories can spend billions manufacturing new cars, but the fact remains — the main reason people buy from us is the sales associate they deal with. And the opposite holds true as well: The main reason people don't buy from us is that they didn't like the sales associate. It's that simple.

That told us that the first thing you must do to be successful in the industry is to get customers to like you. Not the car. Not the dealership. You. When you get people to like you first, the dealership second, and then the car, you will increase your chances of making the sale. I have seen this play out since my first day in the business. The more you get people to like you, the likelier they are to buy from you, and the faster they'll buy from you. You have to make customers feel good, because how they feel is really the basis of a "good deal" — it isn't the price. And people feel good when they are dealing with people they like.

"Rick was just one of those people that everybody liked," John Lanigan says. "He really prided himself in what he did. Rick didn't ever want to give anybody a deal that they were unhappy with. He just wanted to make sure they got the best possible deal."

In other words, people like you when they can tell that you like them and you have their best interests at heart. Those are the kind of people we want on our team.

So this process of getting people to like us really begins with the critical decision of whom to hire. Our philosophy is we prefer not to hire salespeople who have experience selling cars because we don't want to bring in anyone who might carry old — and possibly bad — habits. We prefer to train new sales associates and teach them to embrace our culture of treating every customer as they would their best friend, which is very different from the approach many other dealers take. For example, car salespeople typically don't like to give every customer their home phone and cell phone numbers. They don't like the three-day free trial period we offer, and they don't like the requirement to make two appointments per day by phone before they can talk to a walk-in guest.

I found out many years ago that you can't train personalities. So we hire people first for their personalities, then for their skill set. If they don't want to be contacted by customers after regular business hours, then they won't work with us.

We share these expectations with candidates at the front end of the interview process. Part of the interview process is letting the prospects know about our phone number policy as well as the other non-negotiable policies we have, all of which are designed to benefit the customers. To be honest, many people can't get on board with the way we do things here, and they make the decision themselves that our job isn't for them.

The kind of personality we look for in sales associates we hire is, in a word, positive. They are outgoing and enthusiastic. They are happy with life. They like people, and more importantly, they like helping people. We see this as an "I'm glad I'm here, I'm glad you're here" personality.

How can you determine someone's personality when you first meet? Simple. By listening closely to what people say and how they say it. By analyzing how they act. It's easy to detect when someone has a lot of energy, and usually, a higher level of energy indicates a positive personality. Those people usually seem bubbly, which makes everyone they encounter feel good. For sales positions in particular, this is crucial. When people are happy and upbeat, they're the kind of people you like right away and we have a feeling that they'll treat our customers like their best friends.

Once we've hired the right people who demonstrate the positive attitude we look for, then we train them on our policies and procedures. Our goal is to scale and sustain the successful processes I've developed throughout the past 50 years.

Part of our training for Rick Case associates includes teaching them to pay attention to the details, especially in their approach. Clients start judging as soon as they see you, and that first impression sets the stage for your relationship. How you approach them, your clothing, your personal hygiene, your posture, and your smile all factor in to the impressions you make. We remind associates to think about all of these details. We train them to consider their pace when approaching a customer, the expression on their face (which must include a smile), and how to use a firm handshake when they meet someone. All shirts must be tucked in, and nametags must be attached and straight at all times. We expect associates to pick up any trash they see on the premises, even if that's not necessarily their job, because every one of these details contributes to the overall impression we make. If we miss any one detail, we may not be perceived as the professional operation we are.

During training, we ask associates to think like customers in order to better understand what customers want. We ask them to pull from their retail experiences and think about the types of salespeople that make them most comfortable as customers. They always agree: "We like to buy from people with a great attitude who are genuine, professional, and knowledgeable, who care about us so much they take time to ask questions so they can understand our needs."

And that, of course, is exactly what we aim to deliver. We know those are the essential ingredients that make people like you right away.

Every associate is trained on and receives a copy of the Rick Case Culture card, which serves as a reminder of our philosophy for handling customers and each other. Of the 20 points on the card, here are a few that relate to customer service. These tips, at their core, are designed to get people to like you through our culture of treating every customer as we would our best friend:

• Our mission is to extend genuine, courteous care toward our customers to ensure they return. Display genuine and enthusiastic interest in the customer, and always pay complete attention.

• Smile and greet every customer. Speak to the customers in a warm, friendly manner. Use their names as often as possible. Always use appropriate vocabulary and avoid slang or automobile industry jargon.

• Anticipate customers' needs and be flexible in responding to them. Practice proactive customer service. Pick up on the non-verbal cues to initiate personalized service and "wow" all customers.

• It's everyone's responsibility to learn and honor our customers' preferences so that we can personalize their service.

• Always recognize repeat customers.

• You are empowered and trusted to handle customer needs and problems to the best of your ability. Think of creative ways to say yes.

Although we have training manuals for our sales associates, we remind them that this is not like Hollywood. It's not about reciting lines but rather being genuine. There is no bigger turn-off than a phony. Some people almost expect that from salespeople, especially in the automotive industry, so you can be sure they're on the lookout for it. This is one industry where saying the right thing without sounding real is actually just as bad as saying the wrong thing.

Rick and John Lanigan, Cleveland radio personality, 40 years of friendship

Rick Case
Culture
Treating
every Customer
as we would
our best
friend

Culture Card cover

Chapter 9

Lesson #9: A sales process for a friend

At many dealerships, the sales process starts as soon as the customer pulls on the lot. At those places, eager salesmen instantly approach you. But at Rick Case, our approach is much different.

At our new car showrooms, a manager will greet you — but not until you enter the dealership. Our philosophy is to leave customers alone until they decide they're ready to come inside and talk to us. When they do, that's when the best friend treatment kicks in, which is the foundation for our entire sales process.

During our sales training, we reference a national survey that says less than 15 percent of auto consumers reported that their salespeople did anything to effectively determine their needs. This is a major irritation for customers. It tells them that salespeople don't care about their wants or needs. At Rick Case, our goal is to change that perception — one customer at a time.

We have structured our sales process with that goal in mind. So one of the first things we do is called the "counseling phase," where sales associates find out what customers want and need. Done correctly, this phase will set us up for a successful sale because once you start asking open-ended questions, customers open up more and tell you what they really want. In the process, they usually tell you exactly what it will take for them to purchase from you.

Keep in mind that each customer is different and communicates in a distinct way, which means the way each customer gathers information to make an educated buying decision will vary, too.

We train our team to identify two types of communicators — open and closed — and it's pretty easy to spot the difference. The open communicator is an outgoing, informal, and talkative customer. You can appeal to these types with lots of fast-paced, back-and-forth interaction and testimonials. The close communicators are logical, reserved, and sometimes even defensive customers whose barriers are a little harder to break down. Still, these closed communicators can be won with an organized, systematic approach by an honest salesman who doesn't rely on gimmicks to connect.

In the same vein, there are two types of decision-makers — direct and careful. The impatient, decisive, direct buyer wants quick answers and relies on facts over feelings. Slow, thoughtful, careful buyers need more details, carefully explained. It requires a more patient approach to sell to them.

We train our associates to identify each type of customer through indicators like body language, attitude, characteristics, and even the types of questions they ask. Then, we teach slightly different approaches to communicating with each type. The basics are the same, and it always starts with that counseling process to learn each customer's specific wants and needs. We have learned that the best questions to ask are open-ended, such as, "What do you like about your current car? What would you change? How will the car be used?" The goal is to match an in-stock vehicle to their preferences and remove any obstacles so they can buy and drive today.

Once the associate has collected enough data about the customer's preferences — from body style and features to color and pricing — he leaves the customer to arrange a few cars to look at. But what he leaves with the customer can continue to impact the buying decision. Our "Rick Case Advantages Brochure" and their "Why Buy Here" manual stays behind as a silent salesman that illustrates what sets Rick Case apart. We encourage associates to personalize the manual with their bios and pictures of their families, along with articles and facts about the dealership, testimonial letters, pictures from customers, and product comparisons and our benefits from purchasing at Rick Case.

When they're trying to make a purchase decision, customers will have three critical questions on their mind:

- Does this really meet my needs?

- What will it cost me, in terms I can relate to?

- Am I getting a good deal?

This means that customers will buy when — and only when — you've raised the value proposition higher than the perceived cost. So when we present the product, we "explode" it, highlighting the best features. The associate walks around the car, giving the customer an enthusiastic tour, while keying in on the areas we know that customer is looking for. The big things to hit on during the presentation are comfort, appearance, performance, safety, economy, and dependability. This way, we're selling the car on its value, not its price. Price alone does not sell cars because a "good deal" is how the customer feels — it is a state of mind.

The test drive, or demonstration ride, is such an underestimated part of the process. I've learned the test drive is key, so you can't make it optional. Instead of asking, we say to the customer, "Come on, let's see how you like the way it drives." We even teach our associates certain circuits to drive and spots to stop while they're taking customers on the demo. This ride is an opportunity to prove, in action, the presentation that the associate just delivered.

During the demo ride, we want to help create a scene where the customer can visualize owning the car. We do this by saying things like, "Can you imagine driving this to work every day? What will your neighbors say when they see this car? Where will you take it on your next vacation?" Ultimately, we want to build this up to test where the customer is in the buying process by asking some temperature questions. These can be anything from, "What do you like about the ride?" to, "Isn't this car everything I said it would be?" You're not asking for a decision yet. You're just trying to verify that you're on the right path and to uncover any objections. If their responses are cold, we back up a step to counseling and find another car that may better fit their needs. If they're warm, we keep the focus on the value. And if they're hot, by all means, we concentrate on that selection.

When sales consultants return from the demo ride, the new car never goes back in its original parking spot. Instead, we park the car next to the customer's trade-in or in our "Sold" section. That spot denotes that the car is a pending sale.

Based on the customer's attitude, we move on to a commitment question. This may be as simple as, "Is this the vehicle you would like to own?" Before we talk about buying, we make sure this is the right car. Only then does the manager get involved to help work out the details — but not before we make one more presentation: selling the service department.

The service department is an important stop on the way back from the demo ride to the showroom. When the quality and importance of good service facilities are part of the presentation, it becomes, in the buyer's mind, an important part of the sale. Nothing does more to create repeat business than an effective service department. That gives customers a reason to keep coming back to Rick Case.

Throughout this process, our associates also cover all of the other reasons why customers keep coming back to our dealerships. Besides our best-in-class service department, this includes all of the benefits we offer customers — like doubling the factory warranty, the three-day money-back free trial period, and the opportunity to compare our cars with the competition, right at our dealership. We also explain the additional benefits our customers receive by using their Rewards Card — which gives them access to our discount gas center and free carwashes for life, as well as the opportunity to use their Rewards Points for big savings on future purchases.

Finally, after we've helped the customer find the right car and explained why Rick Case is place to buy it from, it's time for the purchase consultation. We train sales consultants not to ask for a sale without providing all of the tools — things like soft drinks or water, chips, cookies or candy, and toys to keep any kids entertained. Those little touches make people feel comfortable and relaxed. And, even if only subconsciously, it provides the feeling we're looking out for their needs.

With that approach, we can help them narrow down the objections they have to the most important ones. That takes some careful listening and asking more questions to clarify, because the initial concern the customer shares with you might not be the core issue.

"Persuasive without pressure and helpful without force" — that's how one customer described our approach in a very complimentary letter he sent to the CEO of Honda in Japan. In his letter, this customer pointed out that he lives 250 miles away from our dealership, but he makes the trip because of Rick Case's reputation as a fair and honest dealer. Honda's worldwide headquarters in Japan was so impressed by the customer's positive experience that it circulated the letter to all Honda distributors around the world as an example of how all customers should be treated.

In general, people love to buy, but they don't like making decisions. To make sales, you have to help them make decisions in small steps that they can easily agree to. You don't sell by telling; you sell by asking. People buy solutions to problems, where they gain a benefit or avoid a loss. You have to keep asking about their problems and desired benefits so you can position the product as the solution and overcome any obstacles along the way.

It would be nice if we could eliminate objections. But in sales, objections are a fact of life. Our average sales associate addresses five objections before making a sale, usually without even realizing it. We prepare ourselves to handle objections in such a way that we can turn them into opportunities. The most successful mindset a salesperson can have is to welcome objections because they are signs of interest. Objections usually stem from those three primary concerns on a customer's mind when considering a purchase:

- I don't see how these benefits meet my needs.
- I'm afraid that I'm making the wrong decision.
- I don't see the value matching up to the cost.

Another common objection that sometimes keeps customers from buying is financing. This is because more than 90 percent of the people who buy a new car finance or lease it. It's very rare for someone to walk in and present a check in total for a car. People fret a lot about their credit and whether they are able to finance or lease a car in a way that makes it affordable for them. Our attitude has to be that everyone can finance or lease. No matter what the problem is with credit, we will find a solution.

Customers perceive a good deal in terms of how they're treated, how they feel about the experience and the people they're dealing with, and how many unique rewards and benefits they receive. The better you treat customers and the more benefits you can provide — such as doubling the factory warranty and offering free carwashes for life — the more value they perceive.

If we've used the sales process successfully up to this point, it means we've kept working with the customer to overcome any obstacles that might keep them from making a decision — and ideally, making a purchase.

National Dealer Magazine November 2002

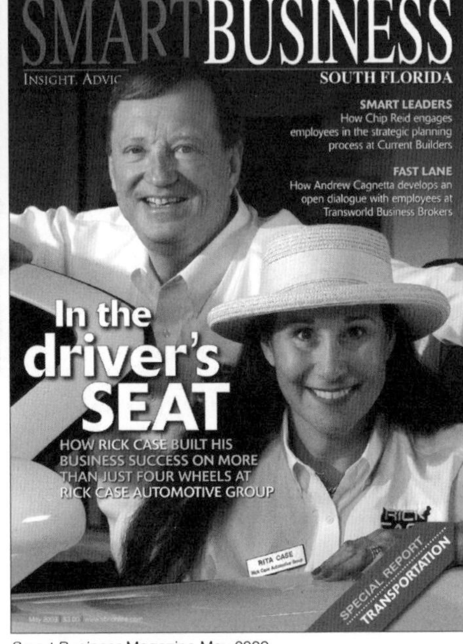

Smart Business Magazine May 2009

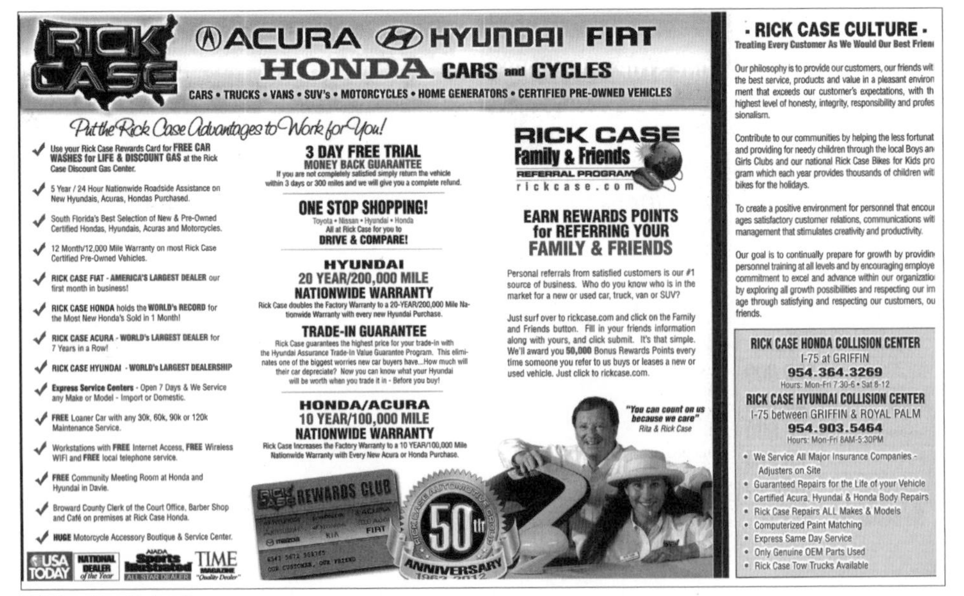

Rick Case Benefits brochure

Chapter 10

Lesson #10: Persistence removes resistance

Many salespeople are afraid to ask for the business because they think it makes them look pushy. But our sales consultants know there's nothing wrong with asking someone to give you the chance to help them when they need it. At Rick Case dealerships, we mandate a certain amount of prospecting to make our sales force proactive about obtaining a sale instead of just waiting for the next customer to walk in.

Here's how it works: Sales associates need to make 20 calls a day in order to speak to 10 people, and our statistics prove that makes two appointments a day. This is our 20-10-2 philosophy.

Sales associates need to hit that quota and have it confirmed by a manager before they can come down to the showroom and help walk-in guests. If they're down in the showroom always waiting for the next guest to come in the door, they can't make those prospecting calls.

The thinking behind this strategy is pretty simple: Prospects and referrals are easier to deal with and, ultimately, to turn into a sale because they're coming with appointments to see a car. You ask them to come in when you can have the most quality time with them, which is usually during slow days or times of the day — Tuesdays, Wednesdays, mornings, or early afternoons. The average sales associate sells one out of every five walk-in prospects but three out of five appointments. The numbers justify our strategy.

Our sales associates don't just leaf through a phone book for their next customer. We utilize a comprehensive database of current customers who have done business with us. That means we start prospecting by calling our current customers.

We want our sales associates to talk to every one of their customers once a month. That kicks in as soon as they make a sale. We have associates follow up with customers who buy a car three, 10, 17, and 30 days after the sale. Then it's every 30 days from there on.

Of course, we always ask customers how things are going with the car they bought from us. However, these monthly calls are much more than product follow-up.

The reason for these calls goes back to the reason we're in business. As I tell my associates all the time: "We're not in the car business — we're in the relationship-building business." We want our associates to call every one of their customers once a month to keep the relationship alive.

When you're persistently treating customers as your best friends, they will buy from you. It's not the other way around. You won't create loyal customers by just focusing on "sell, sell, sell" all the time. When you sell a car, you just sell one car. When you build a relationship, you'll sell many cars.

Even for the best salespeople, it's difficult to call someone up trying to sell something. It's much easier to give them something, so that's what we have our associates do. The reason for the call is not to sell anything — it's to give customers something. Our gifts thank customers for their loyalty with anything from half-price oil changes to restaurant gift cards or sporting event tickets.

This is what we say when we call customers: "Hi Mr. Jones. This is Bob from Rick Case. I hope this is a good time for you. The reason for my call is to let you know how many Rewards Points you've earned: You're up to 185,000. You can use those toward any purchase of vehicles, parts, or service. And to thank you for your business, I'd like to offer you a gift. Stop by this week; I have two tickets to the baseball game set aside for you."

We end these customer calls with a certain line we have ingrained in my associates. We tell them to close every conversation with this line, whether on the phone or in person: "By the way, who do you know that may be in the market for a new or used car or truck?"

It's that simple. By repeating that signature phrase, we make prospecting a way of life for our associates. Statistics show that about 62 percent of customers have family members who will buy a car within 12 months. Many other customers know someone else — a babysitter, a neighbor, or a colleague — who is looking for a new or used car. Fortunately, we're in the type of business where most everyone will need a car at some time. It's only a matter of seeking them out and communicating with them until they buy from you.

The first step is to pick up the phone and call the prospect. The first question we ask is, "Am I interrupting anything?" That's a key courtesy question used in the opening of every call to get someone to like you over the phone.

Then we discuss the prospect's current car by asking questions like, "What do you like about it? What do you want to change? What else are you looking for in a new car?" After that, we have a step called C2: clarify and confirm. C2 ensures we are on the same page with customers so that we're able to meet their needs.

After we've found the right car for the customer, then we have our sales associates talk about our exclusive benefits. They explain how we offer a three-day free trial money-back guarantee, double the factory warranty, and let customers drive and compare the competition at our dealerships. We tell them that Rick Case is the only place where they can earn Rewards Points on every purchase and use those points toward future purchases. We want to let customers know about our benefits because they're so unique. They might find the same car somewhere else, but they won't find these benefits anywhere else.

Then, after associates set up an appointment with the prospect, we train them to give the prospect a reason to ask for them specifically. It goes something like this: "I'll have a few vehicles pre-selected, based on the preferences you've just explained to me." This reminds customers that the associate knows their preferences, so if they went to another salesman or dealership instead of coming to ours, they would be taking a step back. It tells them that we're persistent about treating customers as our best friends.

The final step on the phone call is a simple closing we've designed to increase the appointment show rate. We say, "Do me a favor. If, for any reason, you're going to be early or late to our appointment, please let me know. If anything changes on my end, I'll return the favor. I don't mind waiting for you, but I don't want you to have to wait for me." When you add that accountability, they're more likely to follow through.

Still, not everyone shows up for every appointment. That's where this motto, "Persistence removes resistance," kicks in because we keep asking, keep pursuing, and keep working on making the appointment.

The associate calls the prospect back again, goes through the steps, and tries to get another appointment. If the prospect doesn't set up an appointment, then it's a matter of determining the buying cycle to get a timeline of when the prospect will be ready to buy.

This same motto applies to walk-in customers, too, if they leave our dealership without buying. Within one hour of their departure, one of our managers will call them, and keep calling, until there's an answer. Then they'll say, "Hi, Mr. Jones, we saw that you and your wife were just here in our dealership an hour ago and you didn't decide on a car. What happened?"

Maybe they didn't get enough for their trade, or maybe they had a personality conflict with the sales associate.

"Whatever the reason, we can overcome it," the manager tells them. "Please come back in and we'll work something out for you that will satisfy you."

We end up making sales to 50 percent of our customers who come back that did not buy on their first visit. This is more proof that persistence does remove resistance.

Statistically, we've found that persistence really does remove resistance, because:

- 38 percent of prospects buy within 4 hours
- 57 percent of prospects buy within 3 days
- 90 percent of prospects buy within 1 week

Unfortunately, national statistics show that 91 percent of car salespeople wouldn't know this because they never follow up.

We're relentless about treating customers as we would our best friends. We're persistent about building that relationship first — and selling second — and that's how we create customer loyalty. They know we care more about our relationship with them than the sale itself, and that's why they come in and buy from us. It's why they keep coming back to do business with us — and most importantly, they become raving fans of Rick Case who tell all their family, friends, and business associates how great Rick Case is. Our follow-up also keeps the Rick Case name top-of-mind when customers do need another car or when they hear of someone else who does.

Many businesses think about staying this close to both prospective and current customers, but they just don't have the patience or the persistence to follow through. Most businesspeople simply don't want to take the time or effort to put these programs together, and that's why they continue to be met with resistance. We have learned that the only way to overcome resistance is through persistence.

Rick and Rita Case accept the 2011 Ernst & Young Entrepreneur Of The Year Award

Rick Case presented with the Sports Illustrated Dealer of the Year 1997 by U.S. Senator Bill Bradley

Keith Crain, publisher of Automotive News, presents Rita with the Woman Automotive of the Year Award for 2010

Rita Case receives the National Distinguished Woman's Award from Northwood University President Dr. David Frye, 2005

Rick and Rita receive Outstanding Business Leaders of the Year 2011 from Northwood University

Chapter 11

Lesson #11: Happy associates make happy customers

Because we build long-term relationships with customers and bring them back to our dealerships year after year, it's important that they have the same sales associates and the same management team to come back to time after time. Associate retention builds customer loyalty, because if we retain associates, it means they're happy. If we have happy associates, we're going to have happy, satisfied customers.

The first thing you'll notice is that our word choice represents how we see our team. At Rick Case dealerships, we discourage the e-word. We have associates, not employees. Nobody works for Rick and Rita; everybody works with Rick and Rita.

It's important that we maintain that tone by treating our associates as colleagues. To accomplish this, we do several things. First, our benefit programs are among the best in our industry, with 401(k) plans, health insurance, and four weeks of paid vacation. At our company, your birthday even qualifies as a paid holiday.

But offering benefits is pretty standard across any industry. We stand apart by making real investments in our associates through training and development.

Training is critical because when you can create a single approach to your business — that benefits the customers, the associates, and the company all at once — you align everyone's focus on a single goal. That lays the foundation for everyone to be tremendously successful together.

I have developed several manuals and booklets to guide associates through the process of dealing with customers and making sales. There's even a separate manual for speaking with customers on the telephone. My approach has proven successful over the years, so it only made sense to multiply that success by sharing what I've learned with my team. By doing so, I give my associates everything they need to succeed. Success in any business comes from duplicating proven strategies, not from luck — unless you subscribe to our definition of L.U.C.K., which is Laboring Under Correct Knowledge.

We also send associates to factory training programs, facilitated by manufacturers such as Hyundai, Audi, and Honda, where they learn how to become better technicians or better sales consultants. But we don't stop there. We also invest in the career development of our associates by helping them become better people and better leaders — not just in business.

In 2007, we introduced our organization to Rapport Leadership, an international training program that teaches leadership as a process by helping people understand how to apply effective leadership skills. We refer to it as a leadership experience more than training, and every month we send people to the Rapport Retreat 100 miles outside of Las Vegas, so they are literally in the desert. They return enthusiastic. The program coaches managers on how to become better leaders and promote those leadership qualities to their department associates and customers. We've sent more than 150 associates to the course since 2007, and we continue to enroll associates monthly.

Many leaders give their employees just enough to get the job done, but they don't invest in their development as individuals — and they certainly don't share all of their secrets to success. They're concerned about the risks. But what's the worst that could happen? You might lose them to the competition? That happens. When your employees are the best of the best — and getting better all the time through training — they're going to be in high demand. But so what?

In our case, our associates are sought after in the industry. It is the primary reason why we have any turnover at all —

it happens when another dealer "steals" someone from us. Everybody knows that our associates are well trained in terms of the auto industry, customer satisfaction, and technology. When we lose someone, it's because another dealer is trying to improve his or her business by acquiring our knowledge, skill, and industry know-how. This is a situation most successful, progressive companies face.

Another effect of sharing strategies across a company is that you will spark entrepreneurship in others. Some leaders are concerned about this, so they do not encourage their employees to grow and develop. They do not want to prepare their employees to leave the company and go off on their own.

Sparking entrepreneurship is not necessarily a bad thing. Bill Sander, a longtime manager who began working with me around 1968, decided to take this path after he worked with me for several years.

"When I told Rick I was quitting so I could get my own dealership, he tried to talk me into staying," Sander says. "But when the moment came, he actually came down to Marion, Ohio — located 150 miles away, noncompetitive — and helped me find the location. Once I had committed to do it, he wanted to see me do it. He likes to surround himself with loyal people, and he is as loyal to me as I am to him."

Loyalty is about supporting your associates in whatever ventures will make them successful and satisfied. And simply enough, the loyalty of our associates depends on our loyalty to them. If they feel that we care about them, then they feel invested in the company.

As the owners and personalities behind the dealership, it's important that Rita and I stay visible to associates in order to show our support and appreciation. We can't be in Cleveland and Atlanta at the same time, but there's still a perceived sense of our presence when you walk into any one of our dealerships and see our pictures hanging in several places, or when the associates hand out our business cards with our e-mail addresses and personal phone numbers. These things tell customers that the owners of this dealership are very involved, and it also reminds associates that we are not too far removed from what they're doing.

As the company has grown, it has become more difficult for Rita and I to spend as much time in each store as we used to. We visit the dealerships throughout the year for major meetings and for the annual holiday award celebration.

Thanks to e-mail, we can actually be more present in each associate's life today than we were when we could physically travel more often to the stores. Now, we can communicate with everyone instantly and personally. It's very easy to send an e-mail to our associates to thank them for their contribution or recognize a special accomplishment.

For example, we see every single customer letter that comes into the company. We're sure to recognize the people who provided such great service that they prompted a letter of praise. We'll send personal e-mails thanking the associates for their commitment to treat the customer as their best friend. This way, associates hear from us throughout the month instead of just when we visit the dealerships.

To continue this philosophy year-round, we have instilled traditions — such as our monthly kickoff rallies and our years of service ring program — to help associates feel recognized and appreciated whether we're there to personally thank them or not. As long as our associates honor these traditions we've set in motion, we believe that we will remain present in our dealerships through the culture.

Our company ring program is one way we recognize our associates. Since 1980, we have awarded every associate a company ring on his or her five-year anniversary. Every five years after that, we add a diamond to the ring. It becomes a very visual reminder of the years of service they've devoted to the company and our appreciation of their career commitment.

Another way we appreciate our associates is through the kickoff lunch, which happens at each location on the first Friday of every month. It's basically a big party to celebrate the role our associates play in the company's success. Every associate in the dealership is invited to a catered hot lunch. Each location buys a big birthday cake, iced with the names of all the associates celebrating birthdays that month. The general manager hands out cards, signed by Rita and me, to the associates who are celebrating anniversaries with the company — which are usually in the double digits. They also honor the technician, sales associate, office associate, and the overall dealership associate of the month.

The award winners announced at the kickoffs are also printed in our monthly newsletter, Motorvations. The goal of Motorvations is to publish the names of as many associates as possible so we can recognize their accomplishments. It's also an important communication tool to let our team know what's going on in the industry and, more importantly, their company.

The first page of the newsletter is "News from the Coaches" — those coaches being Rita and me. We discuss industry news as it relates to our business, starting with how Rick Case performed last month compared to the rest of the industry. In September 2009, for example — while most of the industry felt the pain of the recession setting in, with national auto sales only up 1 percent from the previous year — we announced our best month in history, with sales up 54 percent over the prior year. We also use this section to introduce new car models and share other updates from the factories.

The second page of the newsletter is where the name-dropping begins. We announce achievements from the previous month, recognizing the No. 1 overall store, sales, service, and parts winners, and the top sales associates for new, used, and combined sales at each store. We spotlight stores with above-average Customer Satisfaction Index ratings and print photos of each associate who received a company ring in the past month.

At the end of each newsletter, we reprint letters from customers to recognize the associates who made a lasting impression by treating those customers as their best friends. We also include our hotline number so people can call in and recommend company improvements and ideas to us personally.

Through the newsletter, in its 25th year of publication, which now goes directly to each associate and his or her spouse via e-mail, we want to make sure associates know that even though the company has grown and we can't greet each associate every day in the dealerships, we are still closely connected. It's our way of staying in touch and showing them that we work just as hard as they do — if not harder — to secure the company's success, to grow the company for the future, and to stay ahead of the competition.

Even if you have communication tools and recognition programs in place, you can never assume that associates are satisfied just because they continue to perform. You need to keep tabs on how your team feels about their jobs and the support they receive. Communication is the key to understanding this. We conduct confidential, anonymous satisfaction surveys to give associates an opportunity to voice their opinions in an open and honest manner.

Before auto factories even developed the concept of a Customer Service Index in the mid-1980s, we created our own ASI: Associate Satisfaction Index. On the survey, we ask questions like, "How do you feel about the equipment and tools that were provided to you to perform your job?" We want to make sure we're making their jobs as efficient as possible, and we want to give them an outlet for suggestions if they have better ideas. We ask for input on benefits, and we also ask much broader questions, such as, "How do you feel about the management? Do you see this job as a career? If you owned the dealership, what would you do differently to improve it?"

We tabulate satisfaction scores for each store in several areas, from benefits and equipment to communication and support. The goal is to gather ideas on how we can improve the company and to identify areas where we may be falling short. Besides the survey, we train our general managers to recognize satisfaction issues within their teams so they can address an issue before it grows into a real problem.

It comes back to the attention to detail we instill in our team. If an associate is having a bad day, his interaction with a customer could be the only experience that customer has with Rick Case. We constantly remind our team that whatever they do in their facility reflects on the name of Rick Case because all the dealership locations carry that name. Whatever experience the customer has at a dealership is a reflection on the company as a whole. We need to make sure that all of our associates are always happy in order to make every customer happy, every time.

If you have happy associates — who have a career path, a sense of belonging to the organization, and a sense of mission — then you will have happy customers. The way we ensure commitment from our associates is by hiring good managers and training them on our mission and our culture.

"Many businesses — and I've been around a lot of them — don't really train you on what your job is," Sander says. "Rick had job descriptions for people before anybody else in the industry."

Job descriptions always seemed like common sense to me because it is important for your team members to know what you expect of them. It's pretty simple: If you surprise employees with changes all the time, they won't perform as well as if they understand where you're headed and feel just as invested in your mission and culture as you are.

You must be clear about what the company's mission is, and then break down the managers' goals that will help you achieve that. Then, it's not just saying, "OK, you run this store. Go do your thing, and I'll check back with you at the end of the month." You need to keep track of progress constantly to ensure you're moving toward the goals. Managers know we are checking the numbers every day. They know we are always reviewing performance. You must inspect what you expect. That keeps them focused.

In the early days when the business was smaller and it was just me and a few other associates, it was easier to do this because I was working right alongside them. I would challenge them to small sales contests throughout the day, and they would always know what everyone else's sales numbers were. The reasoning behind this was that a dose of peer pressure can go a long way toward motivating performance.

The more you grow in terms of employees and locations, the more you have to make a point of tracking results. As a leader, you will get busier, and daily performance can get lost in weeks or months before you notice a trend. That's why you need to know what's happening in your business in real time — so you can react to it quickly.

As your company grows, you may start tracking different data and delegating some of the monitoring responsibility to others. At first, you keep a close eye on each department. But that will change. You won't be able to run 15 stores by yourself. It's a lot easier to manage 15 managers than it is to manage 1,000 associates, so you pass that responsibility on to the management. This means you need to have good managers in place, tell them your expectations and goals, and then inspect what you expect.

In our case, there came a point where it was more efficient to promote Jack "JJ" Jackintelle to president and chief operating officer, so now each general manager reports to him. Now he makes the daily calls to the managers and checks in with me several times a day.

"At this point in his career, Rick is serving the company better by being my support system than by being there physically doing it day-to-day operationally," Jackintelle says. "If I needed him for two weeks, then he'd be here for two weeks. If things are going fine, he trusts me."

As much as the Rick Case Auto Group has grown, I continue to review daily operating control reports, called doc reports. Wherever I am — even if I'm in California attending dealer meetings — I have that information at my fingertips. I know every statistic at each store, from how many cars were sold to the dollar amount of parts sold. With technology, it's easy to have daily access to the doc report for each dealership.

With any kind of performance review or progress update, you have to approach the associate in a motivating way. I always try to maintain a positive, upbeat manner, and, instead of telling, ask a lot of questions, such as: "What do you think about that?" or, "What do you think you need to do to improve this?"

"Rick always had positive things to say to managers. He always had positive things to say to sales associates," Bob Bartholomew says. "And that trickled down. That type of motivation works. You motivate people by telling them how to get results, and he was the best at doing that."

You try to find good things that people are doing, and you always want to emphasize the positive. These conversations usually include something like, "Good job. You're running ahead of your goal for the month."

But you never want to encourage people to rest on their laurels. So after that, I say something like, "This is good, but don't you think we could be better? How do you think we could sell even more?"

"Our motivation is that we never become satisfied," Jackintelle says. "We just keep on keeping on, and so it leaves little room for complacency. When the month is over, we're already on to the next month — no matter how big it was or what records we set. Our successes are short-lived and short-celebrated, and we're already moving on and raising the bar."

The biggest thing we do to motivate our managers is an idea I came up with 25 years ago. The car business is a one-month business — financial statements come out every month, managers and salespeople are compensated by each month's numbers, bonuses are figured from the month's numbers, and factory incentive programs are set on monthly sales. With a schedule like that, there's a tendency to put off and wait until the last day of the month to bring in business and make sales. To keep my managers steadily productive all month long, I created a weekly managers' contest.

One is a "Fast Start" contest, and then there are four one-week contests. Under this model, there are five month-end closes instead of just one. Each dealership has unique goals based on factors like previous month's performance, available inventory, and benchmarks in their market. For each of the five contests, the store that makes the most progress toward its own goal is the winner. So it's not just about the number of new and used cars sold — it's about the highest percentage of sales toward each dealership's goal. Every weekly contest winning dealership's managers receive a financial reward if their percent is over the goal for that week. That motivates managers to not wait until the end of the month, but to stay at the top of their game all month long. Every week, we email the results to all the managers so they can see where they stand as it relates to all the others stores.

Every month, our newsletter Motorvations comes out and announces the winners of every contest for the month. In that way, we're always rewarding people, not only financially but also through recognition.

Rewarding success — whether through gifts, bonuses, or simple recognition — motivates employees to achieve more.

Rewarding people with carrots is always much more powerful than threatening them with sticks. For us, it's never, "Sell this or you'll be in trouble."

And sometimes, it's not even about the reward itself. If you can create an environment where people feel like team players contributing to a common goal, they'll perform simply for the sake of the team. To that end, enthusiasm goes a long way toward motivating associates when the leader gets so excited about the goal that it excites everyone else.

"Rick Case associates all feel like they're part of the team, and that's a very important thing," Sander says. "A company can only be successful if every person buys in to the philosophy. You need to feel that you're part of the team and that you're contributing toward the common goal. That's the principal thing. Rick gets everybody to sign on with the commitment to do whatever it takes. I think Rick gets the same commitment out of someone to come to work with him that he has to the business."

Helping your associates achieve a goal isn't only about laying out clear expectations, providing them training and tools, and monitoring their progress. Sometimes, they also need a hand.

"My commitment to Rick was, 'I promise you if I'm in too deep, I'll call you,'" Jackintelle says.

Not long ago, I received one of those calls from him.

"I am way behind on the grand opening of the new dealership and some advertising deadlines," he says. "And I called Rick up and said, 'I need you to grab these deadlines and handle them.'"

I told Jackintelle, "Send them over. I got it."

No one will ever get in trouble for asking for help. I always tell associates, "I can't fix a problem that I don't know about." They need to bring it to my attention in order for us to find a solution. Associates know to come to me before small issues become big problems, and that makes life easier for all of us.

"One of the coolest things is that Rick trusts me and he always has my back," says Kerry Becker, who's not even a direct associate but a staff member of the Boys & Girls Clubs of Broward County who has worked closely with Rick Case to organize charity events over the past 15 years. "You're working your butt off to make sure it's a huge success, and the amount of stress is enormous. I can't even tell you how many times I've gone to Rick in tears and said, 'I need your help.' And he's got my back, and he will take over, handle the situation, and make my life so much easier. It's very rare that somebody would do that. If I have a challenge, I can go and discuss it with him and he'll figure out a situation and help get it handled before it becomes an issue. He'll even use it as a teaching opportunity and suggest ways to handle things. Just knowing that he trusts me — it's pretty cool."

That kind of trust is key to long-lasting relationships, inside the company and out. On the Rick Case culture card, which every associate receives as a reminder of our philosophy for treating each other, the first point is: "We practice teamwork and treat each other with the same respect we afford our family and best friend. We adhere to the belief that if we take care of each other, we will be able to take care of our customers." While our motto is to treat customers as our best friends, that treatment has to start with our associates in order for it to trickle down.

RICK CASE AUTOMOTIVE GROUP
COMPANY PHILOSOPHY

CUSTOMERS

TO provide our customers with service of the highest quality, products of the highest value and dealership facilities of the greatest convenience that exceed our customer's expectations while operating with the highest levels of honesty, integrity, responsibility and professionalism.

ASSOCIATES

TO create a positive associate environment that encourages communication with management and stimulates creativity and productivity.

COMMUNITY

TO contribute to the communities in which we do business by providing help for the less fortunate and encouraging cultural growth through our participation with the fine arts and community organizations.

OUR GOAL

TO continually prepare our company for growth by providing associate training at all levels and by encouraging their commitment to excel and advance within the organization, by exploring all growth possibilities. TO respect and treat our customers as we would our best friends.

Company philosophy

MOTORVATIONS

RICK CASE TEAM NEWS FROM THE COACHES — September 2007

Rick Case Honda Cleveland Best Month Ever In 34 Year History

Cleveland Honda/Hyundai Sweeps The August Contest

For the first time ever, we have a clean sweep of the five contests for the August Manager's Contest – Rick Case Honda/Hyundai in Cleveland tag teamed and stole the show! Congratulations to Ken Sidana and Team Members for sweeping the Manager's Contest for the month of August 2007. It was the best month in Rick Case Honda – Cleveland's 34-year history. Congratulations to the entire Rick Case Honda Team and it's team leaders including Ken Sidana, Nels Scafidi, Jason Herron, Ron Maiden, Eric Theis, Steve DiFranco, Don Rohm, Bill Panzarella, Joe Zingale & John Gradomski. Also, for the first time ever, we have a clean sweep of the five contests in August by one dealership. Rick Case Honda/Hyundai – Cleveland teamed up and scored top honors on each of the five contests in August. Again, congratulations to Ken Sidana and his team. GREAT JOB!!

USA Today "Sweet New 08 Accord Does Honda Proud"

In the recent issue of USA Today, James Healey reported on his test drive of the new 2008 Accord. Honda has stretched its mainstay Accord sedan enough that the newly redesigned 2008 model moves up to full size from midsize. It's three inches longer, an inch wider and taller than the previous Accord. Of note: The optional V-6 engine has a cylinder-cutoff feature designed to run on three cylinders, four, or all six. Previously it was a choice between three and six. Honda figures that the new version of VCM, or variable cylinder management, boosts fuel economy one mile per gallon in town, three on the highway vs. the same engine without VCM. Roomy – the extra size isn't wasted. Back seat riders benefit most, getting an inch more extra leg and knee room. There's enough room back there to be comfortable, even when front seats are far back. Most important, though, is that Honda did a sweet job on the overhaul. The combination of pleasant driving, practicality and refinement probably is unmatched among mainstream sedans.

RICK CASE ACURA • PLANTATION

RICK CASE HONDA • DAVIE

SE ZONE'S LARGEST DEALER
YTD 2007
Congratulations **Gian Tosti** & his team!

RICK CASE HYUNDAI • DAVIE

RICK CASE HONDA POWERHOUSE • DAVIE

SE REGION'S LARGEST DEALER
August 2007 & YTD
Congratulations **Rusty Johnson** & his team!

Gwinett Audi Grand Opening

September 1st marked a new milestone in Rick Case history when we opened the first European car franchise, the new Audi dealership in Duluth, GA. Balloons, banners, Audi shirts, business cards and name badges – all were in readiness when we had our first customer come in. They purchased their new Audi in record time not to mention it was two days before the official opening of the dealership. Congratulations to Ralph Cerulli, Tom Greenless and their Team Members for a successful opening. We are all excited about the Team and look forward to being #1 in Georgia by the end of the year.

Jerry Reinhart, Service Mgr. and 1st Audi Service Customer

RICK CASE AUTOMOTIVE GROUP
875 N State Road 7
Plantation, FL 33317

Rick Case Family Picnic

Georgia - October 7th at Collins Hills Park - **Florida** - October 14th at C.B. Smith Park

Motorvations, the monthly associate newsletter

Carol Barbour — Rick Case Enterprises Ft. Lauderdale

Rita, Carol Barbour and Rick

15 Years — Anne Morrocco — Rick Case Hyundai Davie

Rick, Anne Morrocco and Rita

5 Years — Leo Leon — Rick Case Honda Davie

Richard Bustillo, Andy Rada, Leo Leon, Rita and Rick

Enrique Paredes — Rick Case Honda Davie

Enrique Paredes, Mike Bender and Rick

5 Years — John Spicer — Rick Case Honda Davie

Rita, John Spicer, Mike Bender and Rick

5 Years — Scott Goldman — Rick Case Honda Powerhouse Davie

Rusty Johnson, Rita, Scott Goldman and Rick

CSI Shining Stars!

Thanks for being over district in CSI:

Sales - *Hyundai Davie* - **David Smith, Bruce Freiman, Dimitry Yakubovich, Frank Sanchez & team**
Acura Ft. Lauderdale - **Marc Riley, Dayton Diaz, Harvey Becker & team**
Hyundai Bedford - **Corky Allison, Dave Parrish, Robert Fullerton & team**
Mitsubishi Bedford - **Corky Allison, Dave Parrish, Larry Leopold & team**
Hyundai Roswell - **Tom Pacini, Greg Gantner & team**

Service - *Honda Davie* - **Sal Seragusa, Mark Warshefski, Jim Helm, Mike Bender & team**
Hyundai Davie - **Jim Naskrent, Gina Naborre-Kelley & team**
Acura Ft. Lauderdale - **Dave Marshall & team**
Mitsubishi Bedford - **Bob Shippy & team**
Mitsubishi Duluth - **Jonas Lafond & team**
Hyundai Duluth - **Jonas Lafond, Jim Clizbe & team**

Great Job - Congratulations!!!!

5 Years — Tony Stadele — Rick Case Honda Powerhouse Davie

Rusty Johnson, Tony Stadele, Rita and Rick

5 Years — Ruth Marshall — Rick Case Honda Powerhouse Davie

Rusty Johnson, Rita, Ruth Marshall and Rick

5 Years — Olga Amores — Rick Case Honda Powerhouse Davie

Rusty Johnson, Rita, Olga Amores and Rick

Motorvations monthly company ring presentation page

Rapport

LEADERSHIP INTERNATIONAL

SCHOOL OF LEADERSHIP DEVELOPMENT

CERTIFICATE OF COMPLETION

presented to

Rita Case

This is to certify that through your courage and perseverance you have completed

Leadership Breakthrough One

Team # 1808 Date December 14, 2007

Michael A. Saleta, President & CEO

Trainer

Lead—the world will follow!

Rapport Diploma

JFDIN

Rapport's motto JFDIN (just focus and do it now) displayed in Jim Helm's office at the Honda dealership

MANAGERS CONTEST
$2,500

FAST START CONTEST: **TUESDAY, OCTOBER 11TH**
The Managers of the store with the highest percentage of Total Vehicle Gross over **20%** of the #1 Contest attained by **5PM** represented on the MIS will split **$500.**

FIRST CONTEST: **THURSDAY, OCTOBER 13TH**
The Managers of the store with the highest percentage of Total Vehicle Gross over **30%** of the #1 Contest attained by **5PM** represented on the MIS will split **$500.**

SECOND CONTEST: **TUESDAY, OCTOBER 18TH**
The Managers of the store with the highest percentage of Total Vehicle Gross over **40%** of the #1 Contest attained by **5PM** represented on the MIS will split **$500.**

THIRD CONTEST: **TUESDAY, OCTOBER 25TH**
The Managers of the store with the highest percentage of Total Vehicle Gross over **60%** of the #1 Contest attained by **5PM** represented on the MIS will split **$500.**

FINAL CONTEST: **TUESDAY, NOVEMBER 1ST**
The Managers of the store with the highest percentage of Total Vehicle Gross over **90%** of the #1 Contest attained by **6PM** represented on the MIS will split **$500.**

TOTAL WINNINGS OF $2,500 COULD BE YOURS!

The Managers' Contest

Chapter 12

Lesson #12: When you do good things for others, good things happen to you in return

Shopping at Rick Case was a family affair. Because I stocked everything from bicycles and mopeds to motorcycles and cars, I had something for customers of every age. I started them young with bikes, moving them up a size as they grew. All the while, I'd be selling mom her car and dad his motorcycle, too. Other dealerships were just selling cars or motorcycles, one or the other. They didn't think to do anything differently, and that became our competitive advantage. This is why it's so important to think creatively and do the things that others don't do.

I got to see firsthand the excitement of children coming in to buy their first bicycle. I wanted to share that feeling with as many kids as possible. Our wide assortment and big box store appeal also brought in a lot of kids who couldn't afford what they saw.

When I saw all of these children come in and drool over the little red bicycle with the big price tag, I had to do something about it. In 1982, Rita and I responded by creating Rick Case Bikes for Kids. We got the program rolling by donating 100 new bikes to needy children, and then we engaged the community to do the same.

I approached the radio and TV stations I had been advertising with and said, "You know how much money we spend to advertise with you. We have this idea to help needy children receive bicycles, and we want you to help us do that by running this ad for free." By leveraging those relationships we had already built, we even found a camera crew willing to come to our house and donate the filing of a TV commercial.

The TV spot featured Rita and me sitting fireside and a Christmas tree with some bicycles in front of us, with our son Ryan — our daughter Raquel wasn't born yet when we started the program. We would say, "If you have a bicycle you no longer need, no matter what the condition, bring it to any Rick Case location. We'll fix it, and through local charities get it to a needy child in time for the holiday."

This program takes place at the perfect time — when the holiday season is approaching. People are already in the giving spirit, developing a softer spot in their hearts for the less fortunate. We knew a lot of them had bicycles they no longer used sitting in their garages for years. Really, we were helping them out by clearing out their unused bikes and making them feel good about giving. By approaching it from that perspective, we turned Bikes for Kids into a win-win.

This lesson came straight from business, yet worked just as well in the world of charity. In business, I knew, it was all about pleasing the customer — and realizing that customer could also be an associate or vendor or any other party on which you depend. When I realized it was the same way in charity — you had to focus on pleasing the donors as well as the benefactors — I achieved my goals.

Within no time, people started bringing us bikes. Stores like Sears and Montgomery Ward started donating bikes to us. Over the years, it got bigger and bigger to the point we needed help refurbishing all the bikes we received. So we reached out to groups like 4-H Clubs, Rotary Clubs, and even other bicycle shops to help with the workload. As we kept reaching out and expanding the impact, we really turned it into a win-win for the whole community.

We've continued to operate Bikes for Kids every year from Oct. 1 through the holiday season. Since its creation, we have donated more than 100,000 bikes to children who can't afford them.

The whole reason behind this is to help the children. Like all good deeds, it comes back to reward us in other ways that we didn't originally intend.

"In addition to his promotional talent with the concepts that he came up with, what set Rick apart was his commitment to the community," says Tom Gruber, whom I worked closely with when Wayne Huizenga was forming AutoNation with Gruber as his chief marketing officer. "For years, he has been collecting bicycles at Christmastime and having them reconditioned and providing them to youngsters that couldn't otherwise afford bicycles. That's a small thing, but those ideas grew and became more grand and he got behind major community projects to the point where now, Rick and Rita are as well known in the communities where they operate for their philanthropy as they are for the car dealerships. By the way, that doesn't hurt car sales. The more contacts they make, the more people that he touches, the more they trust him — they're going to buy a car from him.

"If you build it, they will come," Gruber continues. "And that's what Rick is doing. Although you might find a Rick Case Acura car he donated to a Boys & Girls Clubs activity, he totally dissociates his business from charity. He really just deep down does believe in the philanthropic projects that he gets behind. And when he gets behind them, he comes up with all kinds of new and innovative ways to do it."

That kind of branding is an example of the good that has come back to us without any intention on our part. For example, people have told us, "You do a lot of great things for the community, and you do this program for the poor kids who can't afford bikes. I'm going to buy my car from you guys because I want to support that."

We never do philanthropic deeds because they will benefit the business. We truly believe in and are committed to charity. We get involved because we want to help people who are less fortunate than us. Then you find out that the more you do, the more people begin talking about you.

Newspapers run stories. TV stations cover events. And all of a sudden, your good deeds take on a life of their own. People begin to say, "Well, why should I buy a car from anyone else when the Cases are doing so much to support the community?"

We don't participate in any charity event to help our company. We have plenty of other ways to help our company with exclusive promotional ideas and customer benefits that no other dealer in the country offers. We get involved with charity because we want to and we can — meaning not many people have the combination of creative ideas, energy, capacity, and a willingness to sacrifice their time to pull off an event that doesn't directly benefit their business.

Believe me, good will come back to you in ways you can't even imagine. In our case, the mayors in each of our markets have even proclaimed a day in December as the city's official "Rick Case Bikes for Kids Day" every year for many years.

It just goes to show that when you do something good for other people, good things will happen to you.

Rick Case is chiefly responsible for creating and executing one of the Boy's Clubs' most profitable fund-raisers, the Cat Cay Rendezvous, a yachting excursion to be held Nov. 2-5, featuring fishing, golf, tennis, a casino and, this year, the 284-foot *Trump Princess.*

Rick Case:

Steering kids in the right direction

By LAURIE BROOKINS
Society East Writer

PROFILE

Yes, you could buy a used car from this man — and probably should, not only because Rick Case is one of the largest auto dealers in the U.S., but because his affable personality leads one to instantly trust this dynamic superdealer.

Born and raised in Akron, Ohio, Case officially got his start in the automobile trade at the age of 15, when he purchased his first car, refurbished it and then sold it for a $400 profit, which, he says, "was about equal to what I'd made all year with my paper route, so I figured this was the thing to do."

After selling retail and wholesale cars during high school and college, Case opened his first lot, a retail used-car lot in Akron, and, he says modestly, "it just grew from there."

Did it ever — Case now boasts 10 dealerships throughout the U.S. and is a member of the Superdealers Group, founded by J.D. Powers and Associates and consisting of the country's top 100 auto dealers.

But while every moment of his day is planned, every hour scheduled, Case finds the time to take on two other projects close to his heart — the Boys Clubs of Broward County and Cat Cay, a private island 54 miles east of Fort Lauderdale and 12 miles south of Bimini.

In fact, Case has found a way to combine the two with the Cat Cay Rendezvous, an annual three-day yachting weekend to be held Nov. 2 - 5 to benefit the Boys Clubs.

The rendezvous got its start two years ago when the Boys Clubs of Broward County found themselves with a major budget deficit, and Boys Club Executive Director David Hughes approached his board of directors — of which Case is a member — for help.

"Rick was just amazing," says Hughes. "He took our problem as a challenge and came up with a prospectus for four different fund-raising events." Case had plenty of experience in this endeavor, as he's either chaired or co-chaired each of the Boys Clubs' two major fund-raisers, the Honda Classic golf tournament and the annual Dinner Auction.

"Now, you have to understand," adds Hughes, "this prospectus was really a beautiful package, very detailed — no one had ever presented us with anything that intricate."

The Boys Club board chose Cat Cay from the package — Case, of course, chaired the event, and the first year out raised $80,000.

"Most fund-raisers lose money the first year," contends Case, "so to clear $80,000 is a real accomplishment." For his efforts, Case received the Boys Clubs' highly coveted Five-Star Award, which, says Hughes, "we've only awarded four other times. It's a prestigious honor for those who have contributed significant new things for the Boys Clubs."

Case hopes to top last year by just a small margin, with a goal of $500,000. But he makes you believe he'll do just that — with a schedule of events to include golf, tennis and fishing tournaments, the presence of the largest yacht in the U.S., the 284-foot *Trump Princess*, a Monte Carlo Night sponsored by Donald himself (yes, he might be there, hints Case), cocktail parties and luncheons, the weekend is truly a chance to relax and hob nob a la *Lifestyles of the Rich and Famous.*

And Case is quick to point out that a *yacht* is not a requirement for attending. "No boat is too small," says Case. Also, while boat owners of all shapes and sizes from around the country have committed, Case hopes that Broward boaters will come through as the major participants.

"While we're getting all wrapped up with the excitement this event is generating," says Case, "we have to remember that our mainstay of participants are the people of Broward County, the ones we count on to make this a success." One reason for the na-

“ [Rick] is the kind of guy you dream of having for a board member — a dynamic guy who sees a problem and takes the steps to solve it. ”

— David Hughes,
Executive Director
Boys Clubs of Broward County

See Case, page 9

Story in the South Florida Sun Sentinel in 1989 about the Boys Club and Rick's charity events

Case

Continued from page 4

tional recognition is the enthusiasm exuded by Jeff Hammond, publisher of *Power and Motoryacht* magazine, who attended last year. Hammond got such a kick out of the event that he gave it a super review and promptly committed himself as a major sponsor this year.

The main reason for Hammond's exuberance is Cat Cay itself — an island paradise that boasts miles of beach, a beautifully groomed nine-hole golf course and a 115-slip marina. Case has had quite a hand in the restructuring of Cat Cay, which, with two other investors, he purchased recently from Al Rockwell of Rockwell International.

However, Rick Case, Island Owner, doesn't exactly have time to sit back and enjoy the view.

"After an 11-hour board meeting on Saturday," says Case with a laugh, "we are discovering that owning an island is a lot of work." Currently underway is the construction of a new airport, complete with 2,450-foot runway, and the expansion of Cat Cay's telephone system, heretofore consisting of about three lines on the whole island.

Which doesn't stop Case from constantly visiting the island, usually on one of his three boats: a 66-foot Pacemaker yacht, *Number One*, his fishing boat, the *Cat Cay Fishing Team*, or the *Cat Cay Express*, a 38-foot cigarette — which, says Case, "I use to go back and forth to Cat Cay; I can make the trip in about an hour."

And Case contends that there's no better getaway for him and his family, which includes his wife, Rita, and their two children, an eight-year-old son named Ryan and a five-year-old daughter, Raqual.

Finally, when Case says he's getting away from it all, he's not kidding around — no cars are allowed on the island, and transportation is strictly by foot or golf cart.

While Case's involvement with the Boys Clubs initially started through the Honda Classic, his commitment has extended far beyond the professional.

"I feel very strongly about the drug problem, especially in this area of the country," says Case.

"The kids in these areas need something to do," he adds. "It's when they don't have something to do that they get involved with the wrong things and the wrong people. The Boys Clubs give them something to do, keep them off the streets and keep their minds occupied with positive things."

“ The Boys Clubs give the kids in this area something to do — they keep them off the streets and keep their minds occupied with positive things. ”

— Rick Case

Always one to set a good example, Case's mind is now occupied with many positive projects: the Cat Cay Rendezvous, with 30 boats currently committed (Case expects about 50 more boats to get in on the fun); his new Infiniti dealership, scheduled to open in January of 1990 in Pompano Beach; and, finally, a new project for the Boys Clubs, an antique and classic car show and auction (what else?) that Case is coordinating with renowned car collector Tom Lester. His first planning meeting for that event will be held Tuesday.

So Case has come a long way since the boy with the paper route and refurbished car — perhaps his own success is a primary reason for his desire to "steer these kids in the right direction."

★ ★ ★

Spaces are still available to participate in the Cat Cay Rendezvous. Fees are $2,500 for one boat, which includes four participants and covers the costs of boat registration, meals and activities. Additional guests or non-boaters are $500 per person, and rooms are available for $750 per couple for all three nights.

For more information, contact David Hughes at the offices of the Boys Clubs of Broward County at 561-2697.

Bikes for Kids poster

Proclamation

WHEREAS, 29 years ago, the "Bikes for Kids" program was started by Rita and Rick Case in conjunction with the local Boys and Girls Clubs and other local charities to distribute new and pre-owned bicycles during the holiday season to those children whose holiday may be less than bright; and

WHEREAS, this program teaches kids a valuable lesson about the joys of giving as well as providing a much appreciated gift for children who might otherwise not hope to receive such a present; and

WHEREAS, throughout the program's history, more than 100,000 bikes have been donated in Cleveland, Atlanta, and South Florida; and

WHEREAS, this contribution is significant in terms of effort and spirit by all who participate in this worthwhile project; and

WHEREAS, it is hoped that 10,000 more bicycles will be received and given to deserving children this year;

NOW, THEREFORE, I, Rae Carole Armstrong, Mayor, and the City Council of Plantation, Florida, do hereby proclaim Wednesday, December 8, 2010, as

"Rick Case Bikes for Kids Day"

in the City of Plantation and commend these hard-working young people and Rita and Rick Case for their unselfish dedication to this program, and encourage our residents to support this outstanding project in every way possible.

IN WITNESS WHEREOF, I have hereunto set my hand and caused the Seal of the City of Plantation to be affixed this 8th day of December 2010.

Rae Carole Armstrong, Mayor

Example of a City Proclamation for Rick Case Bikes for Kids Day

Rita and Rick Case celebrate their Bikes for Kids program at the Rita and Rick Case Boys & Girls Club in Davie, Florida

Chapter 13

Lesson #13: Don't be afraid to be first

In 1983, Honda became the first Japanese manufacturer to announce it was coming out with a luxury brand. Because we were consistently the largest Honda dealers in the country, Honda offered us the opportunity to open a dealership anywhere in the country to start selling this new car called Acura.

We knew this was a great opportunity. We had seen Honda's success in the economy class firsthand since the brand came to the U.S., so we were sure Honda would be just as successful in the luxury market. Plus, we were excited to have the opportunity to build its presence in that market segment from the ground up.

Rita and I researched the market and identified that Southern California and South Florida were the two best markets in the country for Mercedes and BMW, the only import luxury cars sold in America at that time. Both areas represented the high income per capita and the melting pot of cultures that were needed to create a sustainable demand for high-end import cars.

We were already familiar with the South Florida area, and it helped that Florida was in the same time zone as our other dealerships. We chose a centralized location in Broward County that put us within an hour of 4 million people. The way I saw it, we were moving toward growth opportunities. In May 1985, we broke ground for the world's first Acura dealership.

The move was designed to further expand our car business. I could see the writing on the wall with the motorcycle business. Baby Boomers were aging. The price of motorcycles was rising, as were insurance rates. Considering all of those factors, the motorcycle business no longer held the allure it once did, which for me translated to "less volume," and I'm a volume guy. The opportunity for high-volume sales was all but gone, so we sold all 14 of our Ohio motorcycle dealerships in 1985 and moved our corporate headquarters to Fort Lauderdale, Florida, with the goal of expanding in the southeast.

That left five car dealerships in Ohio — Honda and Isuzu in Akron and and Honda, Mitsubishi, and Isuzu in Cleveland — which I left under the control of the general managers, who continued reporting directly to Rita and me.

As we were buying the land and designing the drawings to build the Acura store in Florida, we began to hear murmurs throughout the industry about South Korean carmaker Hyundai entering the U.S. market.

Hyundai had started selling cars in Canada and became a big success story there. Naturally, we wanted to get in on the ground floor of this import's success in the U.S.

Rita and I flew to Hyundai's offices in Toronto to discuss the brand's move to the U.S. with Hyundai's Canadian president, Mr. Park. We visited the dealerships, drove the cars, talked to the dealers, and did our due diligence to understand the company's future growth potential. We were impressed with the car as well as the Canadian dealers' investment and confidence in the brand and product.

I have some very straightforward criteria when it comes to investing in a new brand for our company. For me to consider it, it must have the potential to be a volume brand that appeals to the masses. That usually means it's affordable, reliable, and fuel-efficient. We always look for import cars. The Koreans already had a reputation for producing an efficient, quality product. Hyundai was the largest shipbuilder in the world and the largest company in South Korea, so I knew they had the staying power to support the introduction of a new brand in the United States. This car would sell for $4,995, which was by far the lowest price on the market.

Rita and I wanted this franchise as soon as it came to the country, and at 13 acres, the property we had secured for the Acura dealership was large enough for two dealerships. By then, we were accustomed to pioneering new products — similar ones like Honda, Isuzu, and Toyota. We knew we could be successful with Hyundai, too, especially after seeing how well it was doing in Canada. We had the location and the experience to proceed with the introduction of the new Korean car.

Once Hyundai opened its U.S. offices in California, I called the company to see about getting a dealership. During the discussion, Hyundai's U.S. executives said they would only consider awarding franchises to big-name dealers who had been dominant in their local market for years. Because I was new to Fort Lauderdale — actually, I wasn't even in business there yet — they said, "You can't have it. You've never sold cars in Florida before. Nobody knows you. We only want the biggest dealers who have been in the market for a long time."

As usual, I wouldn't take no for an answer. I assembled a package that was designed to convince them otherwise, and flew out to meet with the Korean and American executives of Hyundai. There was Max Jamieson, formerly of Toyota, whom Hyundai hired to run their American car business. He brought Art Meissner with him from Toyota to be Hyundai's national sales manager. The meeting also included Rick Caille, Hyundai's dealer placement manager, who previously worked for Honda and knew my track record of success with that franchise.

Throughout the presentation, I outlined our previous successes and explained the types of offers we'd promoted at Rick Case dealerships — things they'd never heard of a dealer doing before, like the 10-day free trial money-back guarantee and the gas mileage guarantee.

I explained to them how I came up with "Dare to Compare," and that I'd use the same tactic to launch Hyundai, letting customers drive and compare the car with the competition at our Hyundai dealership.

Everything I talked about underscored one common theme: Hyundai needed somebody new to the scene to shake up the market, and I stressed that I was the one to do that in South Florida.

Going into that presentation, I adopted the attitude that I was going to get this done, make it happen, and not take no for an answer. The attitude during any negotiation is important. The first step, as always, is selling yourself before selling the idea by getting people to like you. Then, the most important part of making your case is the preparation — assembling all of the books and binders and TV and radio spots that build the case that they can't turn down. Then, it's selling them with passion and persistence until they're convinced.

We spent the entire day in that boardroom, going back and forth in our discussion. Them telling me it wasn't going to happen; me laying out my case. In the end, my preparation paid off. The presentation impressed Hyundai's executives so much that they didn't just give me the Hyundai franchise in South Florida; they wanted me to take a larger role in their U.S. expansion.

They said, "You've convinced us that we need somebody like you, and we want you to have one of the biggest markets in the country. You have the Atlanta franchise, as well."

Gwinnett County, in the Atlanta market, had been the fastest-growing county in the country for three years in a row. I didn't even have to ask for it; it just came as part of the deal.

We opened the first two Hyundai dealerships in the country in February 1986 and the first Acura dealership in the country in March that same year. The Rick Case Auto Group expanded by its biggest bounds yet with an $8 million expansion southward. The joint Acura/Hyundai dealership in

Fort Lauderdale, alone, was an investment of more than $5 million. It would pay off though — I knew the additions would boost our sales by more than $50 million in 1986.

We didn't let the idea of being in three different states affect our confidence that we could succeed across the geographic challenges — extensive travel, long workdays, and a seven-day work schedule. And we certainly weren't going to turn down an opportunity that we hadn't even requested. Our goal was to be No. 1, and anything less was not an option.

Once I got the Hyundai dealership, another challenge lied ahead: pioneering another new product, the first Korean car ever sold in the United States. We had to explain to customers that, yes, Korean cars could be reliable — but first, we had to explain how to properly pronounce the car's name. There were at least seven different ways people were trying to say Hyundai. I made it really simple: Hyundai rhymes with Sunday, pronounced "Hun Day".

As I told the Hyundai executives I would do, I used the "Dare to Compare" concept as part of our introduction strategy. I bought a new 1986 Toyota, Honda, Chevy, Ford, and Nissan for people to drive and compare with the new, better Hyundai.

And I did the same thing when the Acura dealership opened. Nobody had ever heard of a Japanese luxury car, so I bought a new Mercedes, BMW, and Cadillac to compare on the Acura lot, and I invited people to come see for themselves that Acura was a better value with equal or better performance and features.

Within the first month of business, we became the largest Acura dealer and the largest Hyundai dealer in the country by sales volume. It was always our goal to sell or lease every Acura for less than any other dealer. But it is our commitment to treat every customer as we would our best friend that has made us the "World's Largest Acura Dealer" for seven years running.

In December 2000, we set a world sales record by selling more new Acuras in a month — 307 — than any other dealer. We eclipsed that record one year later by selling 379 Acuras in one month, and we still hold that record today. We outsold the four other Acura dealers in the Miami-Fort Lauderdale market combined, outselling the next best dealer by more than seven times. We also set the record for selling 2,515 Acuras that year, the most sold annually by any dealer since Acura was introduced. We also received J.D. Power & Associates' customer satisfaction award at Acura. It just goes to prove that volume sales and customer satisfaction go hand-in-hand.

The first Rick Case Acura ad, March 1986 in Fort Lauderdale

The first Rick Case Hyundai ad, February 1986 in Fort Lauderdale

Rick Case Hyundai, Fort Lauderdale, Florida, 1986

The first 2 Hyundai dealerships to open in the U.S. February 1986

Rick Case Hyundai, Atlanta, Georgia, 1986

Ground breaking ceremony, May 1985 for the first Acura dealership in the U.S., later to become the largest volume Acura dealership in the world.

Rick Case Acura, Fort Lauderdale, Florida, 1986

Chapter 14

Lesson #14: Apply business skills to philanthropy

When we moved to South Florida, our reputation preceded us — and it didn't all revolve around cars. News of Rick Case Bikes for Kids had spread through the local charities. Shortly after our arrival in Fort Lauderdale, we were approached to join the community efforts.

The national Honda Golf Classic — formerly known as the Jackie Gleason Classic — was a big draw in Fort Lauderdale. The event benefited the Boys & Girls Clubs of Broward County, Florida. One of the Honda staff who knew about our philanthropic efforts up north told the head of the Boys & Girls Clubs to seek us out.

"Rick and Rita Case are coming to town," he told then-Executive Director David Hughes. "You better grab them before somebody else does because they did a lot of philanthropy work in Cleveland. They could really help you out."

So Hughes called to arrange a meeting.

We met in a small, back office of my new dealership because my office wasn't yet completed. At the meeting, Hughes asked if I would consider contributing to the Boys & Girls Clubs. I agreed. Then, after about a year of making donations and working with the organization through its Honda Classic, I was asked to join the board.

"It was difficult to get on our board because we had a very strong board, and it was very selective," Hughes remembers. "At that time, we were getting hardly anything from anybody except from our board efforts. The organization was relatively small at that time: We had three clubs and our budget was less than $1 million a year. After about a year of involvement, the nominating committee asked if Rick would consider coming on the board."

When I was asked to come on the board, the organization was facing a challenging year and a budget deficit. I came prepared to help.

"I'll never forget the first board meeting Rick came to," Hughes remembers. "He walks in with binders — three bound proposals for fundraising events for us to look at. He had it all organized: What it would entail, what it would create, and it was all very professionally done. We chose the boating event."

The boating event was a no-brainer. Entrepreneurs know how to identify needs and develop creative solutions. The best solutions fill multiple needs at one time. I looked at the organization, its needs, and the resources available around Broward County. My idea was a Yachting Rendezvous.

Fort Lauderdale is the yachting capital of the world. I knew this because I have been an avid boater since saving up enough money from my newspaper route to buy my first boat, and when I moved to South Florida, I could hardly wait to take advantage of the location. So I wondered what the yachting industry could contribute to the Boys & Girls Clubs of Broward County and what those businesses could get in return.

Our family also owned a home on Cat Cay — an island in the Bahamas — where we were stockholders and I was a member of the executive committee of this private island. From that perspective, I could also identify opportunities for the island to donate to and benefit from the event. With that, I had the location of the first Yachting Rendezvous.

When you keep your eyes open to look for creative ways to solve the problems around you, you'll see a lot of possibilities. In this case, I saw a triple opportunity to serve the yachting industry, the island, and the Boys & Girls Clubs — all at once — because I kept my eyes and ears tuned to the needs around me and then applied creative problem-solving to meet them.

The goal of any charity event is the same as any goal you have in business — to treat customers as your best friends and meet all of their needs. And just like in business, you must think of your customers in terms beyond just the people who buy cars from you. At Rick Case, we also treat our vendors and the factories as best friends. In this case, the customers were the participating yacht owners and yachting businesses. And the vendors, so to speak, were the Boys & Girls Clubs of Broward County and the island of Cat Cay. My goal was to make the Yachting Rendezvous a win-win-win for all three groups.

In order to make an event a win-win for everyone involved, you have to be able to think about it from every possible angle — just like you must try to see things from each customer's perspective in a business transaction. The Yachting Rendezvous would help the island by bringing people out to experience it and become members. It would give the industry a boost by allowing businesses to participate, selling anything from yachts to yachting magazines, to a captive audience of yacht owners. And all of this was done to raise money for the Boys & Girls Clubs.

One of my philosophies in doing charity events is to always look for opportunities that benefit other businesses. I knew if I could help them, they would help the charity. Through their involvement, they would be able to expose their products and share their message with the participants. That provided them with much needed funds from the event. By paying sponsorship fees and getting participants to come to the event, they were delivering value to the Boys & Girls Clubs of Broward County.

This concept was embraced by the board and staff at the Boys & Girls Clubs, and has been ever since.

"One of the most important things that Rick has taught me when working with sponsorships is to look at what the companies and businesses are going to get out of their sponsorships and how can we make it work for them," says

Kerry Becker, director of corporate events for the Boys & Girls Clubs of Broward County. "It's sad to say that most people honestly don't care as much about the charity as you'd hope they would. So that's something Rick has really put into play: How can we increase your sales? How can we give you guys the most bang for your sponsorship dollars?

"And that has made us a success. There are probably 100 charities in town that do events all the time. We set ourselves apart because we care about our guests and we care about our sponsors, and that's because of Rick's vision. He knows, as a businessman, what makes him happy and what a good investment is sponsorship-wise, so he wants to see the same thing for other companies that are involved in the different events that we do."

The first year that we held the Yachting Rendezvous, we had six yachts in attendance and raised about $80,000 — which was a lot at that time. Each year the event grew. By its fourth anniversary, the Yachting Rendezvous had become the world's largest charity yachting event. It became so big that we had to move it from Cat Cay to Fisher Island in Miami to accommodate more yachts.

Over the years, this event has netted anywhere from $1 million to $4 million each year.

"It had a huge, huge impact and kind of changed our whole path for the Boys & Girls Clubs," Hughes says. "It took us more toward the special event fundraising mode for targeted audiences."

In other words, the Yachting Rendezvous wasn't an event that just anybody would or could attend. By introducing this concept, we had begun to target certain interests and demographics. And, because we targeted a wealthy group, we could charge significant ticket prices and higher-end sponsorships — with all of that additional money benefiting the Boys & Girls Clubs.

Throughout the event, we coordinate entertainment and events to give our guests a good time. On Thursday, the first evening, we hold a yacht hop, which is a progressive dinner and cocktails from yacht to yacht. On Friday night, we have a themed party — which over the years has featured themes such as the '50s, Polynesia, western, disco, pirates, and Mardi Gras.

Throughout the weekend-long Rendezvous, we provide everyone with plenty of additional opportunities to make donations. The silent auction starts at noon on Thursday and continues until Saturday evening. We take the final silent auction bids as the cocktail party kicks off on Saturday night. Then, during the formal gala dinner, we hold a live auction where people bid on the big-ticket items such as private vacation homes, yacht charters, and walk-on roles on TV shows.

This all leads up to the main entertainment that night. For our 20th anniversary, we featured The Village People, Gloria Gaynor, and The Pointer Sisters. Little Richard, Michael Bolton, and KC and the Sunshine Band have also performed at the event. In 2011, The Doobie Brothers performed. The year before that, we featured The Blues Brothers: Dan Aykroyd and Jim Belushi. Jim Belushi even donated an auction item that year — a walk-on role on his television show, "The Defenders."

Naturally, because this became such a high-profile event — and a successful one at that —we've attracted such guests over the years as Oprah Winfrey, Henry "the Fonz" Winkler, Evander Holyfield, and Arnold Schwarzenegger. Since 2009, Donald Trump and his wife have served as honorary chairs and invited all the Rendezvous guests to their private club, Mar-a-Lago, in Palm Beach.

In 1999, the Rendezvous was named the most successful fundraiser for the Boys & Girls Clubs anywhere in the country. The Rendezvous continues today, every November, raising more than $30 million over the years for the Boys & Girls Clubs. In 2012, we will celebrate the event's 25th anniversary.

This event has multiplied its success by sprouting ideas for other events. One thing we began noticing at the Rendezvous is that a lot of the yacht owners also owned Harley Davidsons. They had bikes on the decks of their yachts, so we saw another opportunity. I told the board that we should do another event that plays off the motorcycles.

In 1995, at the eighth annual Yachting Rendezvous, NASCAR driver Kyle Petty led a parade of guests on their motorcycles to center stage, where they announced the first Biker's Ball. This was a charity event designed for motorcycle enthusiasts and the motorcycle industry.

We held the Biker's Ball in Daytona during Bike Week every March. It was so successful that we decided to also do one in Fort Lauderdale. We called this one the Biker's Bash.

It attracted high-end bike builders and national magazines, Hughes recalls. "They were the right kind of people who could write big checks. The custom bike builders would build custom bikes and donate them to us for our live auction. It just kind of snowballed, and that became another big event for the Boys & Girls Clubs."

After these two successes, I began to think about the other large industries in Florida, because each represented an opportunity to partner up and help the Boys & Girls Clubs. Real estate was big in the late '90s, so I thought it made sense to create an event that could generate revenue from the real estate market.

As with the others, I focused on helping as many groups as possible with a single event. Thus, we created Ship and Shore, which benefited yacht brokers, real estate brokers, and car dealers.

Here's how it worked: We would serve a progressive dinner at very high-end houses that were on the market. At each house, there would be cars for sale in the front yard and yachts for sale at the dock in the back. That triple sale — houses, yachts, and cars — didn't just engage a lot of brokers; it brought in a lot of buyers.

"It got us out there," Hughes says. "It generated a lot of money and let us meet a lot of people who could help us in other ways. It was always all about getting to people who could become believers in the cause and could donate in other ways. The people that came to Ship and Shore, the Rendezvous, or other events that we created would become donors far beyond just buying a ticket to the event. They would give us auction items, and we ended up naming clubs after several people because they gave so much money. It was all part of opening the doors to the affluent society — not only in Fort Lauderdale but all around the country — who could support us, and giving them something in return because they had fun at the events."

This concept of bringing people in and building loyalty mirrors what we've done at the Rick Case Auto Group for years. We're always trying to promote our brand and expand our offerings in order to bring in more customers. If we could get them to come in for a motorcycle, they became a potential customer to buy a new car. The same goes for charity events. If you can get someone to come to an event to see The Doobie Brothers perform, then it's possible to further engage them to contribute to the organization in bigger ways later.

Five years after I moved to Fort Lauderdale, I heard that Broward County was going to build a convention center. This screamed opportunity to me, because Fort Lauderdale is one of the top auto markets in the nation — and they didn't have an auto show. This new convention center would be the perfect opportunity to start one.

I went to the county and was able to get them to award me the rights to the Fort Lauderdale International Auto Show. Then I assigned those rights to the Boys & Girls Clubs of Broward County, which meant they owned the event, and I would be its founder and run it. Together, we were in a good position because this arrangement meant that nobody else could do a car show in that convention center.

Then I got anxious. It was 1990, and I was excited about the auto show. The convention center was still a year away from completion, so I improvised and put on a show at the existing Galleria Mall, one of the biggest malls in the area. We held the International Motor Fair in the parking deck, and the Sun-Sentinel newspaper sponsored it. The extravaganza featured a collector's car auction, a classic car show, a new car show, and an antique car parade that stretched from Boca Raton to Fort Lauderdale.

This event set the groundwork for a more fine-tuned, full-blown auto show when the convention center opened.

"By the time the convention center was done, we were in a position to go to auto show producers and get them to bid on it," Hughes recalls. "We could say, 'What would you give for us to partner with you to produce this auto show in Fort Lauderdale?'"

We picked the one that we thought was the best and struck a deal.

"It was just unbelievably incredible," Hughes says. "There was no downside, no expense at all. Every penny was fronted by the show producers."

Fort Lauderdale didn't have an auto show of any kind, and now it has every kind of car show rolled into one: a new car show, an antique and classic car show. Factories have new autos on display while collectors showcase unique classic cars — like the 1986 white Ferrari that Don Johnson drove in "Miami Vice."

The Fort Lauderdale International Auto Show has been a huge success. It generates hundreds of thousands of dollars annually, totaling more than $5 million over the past 20 years — all benefiting the Boys & Girls Clubs of Broward County.

When it comes to our most successful and best-known car-related charity event, I can't take credit for the idea. I literally copied it after the Pebble Beach Concours d'Elegance in California and the Meadowbrook Concours in Michigan. In 2007, I started the Concours d'Elegance in Boca Raton. Concours d'Elegance is a French phrase, literally meaning "competition of elegance." These events feature a contest where vehicles are judged on excellence of appearance.

"You keep wondering, 'When is he going to run out of ideas?'" Hughes says. "And I don't think that's going to happen. He comes up with this idea for a high-end classic car show called Concours d'Elegance and says, 'This is going to be bigger than anything we've done. It's going to be bigger than the Rendezvous.' Everybody thought, 'Well, OK, we'll see. How are you going to be bigger than the Rendezvous?' But he pulled it off. It's just incredible."

We achieved success with the Concours because we didn't try to reinvent the wheel. Rita and I researched the idea by visiting other Concours events, including Pebble Beach. We met with the directors and learned the best way to handle every aspect of the event, educating ourselves on how to do things right. It was akin to the type of due diligence we did for each auto brand before agreeing to add a new dealership.

After our investigation, we learned how necessary fine food and wine were at a classic car show. That pointed us toward partnering with local restaurateurs and wine distributors. To be successful, you must understand your clientele and ensure every detail is tailor-made to be over-the-top perfect for their preferences. You want the impact to be so powerful the first year that they say, "Wow, we can't wait to get involved again next year."

Our Concours is a three-day event that kicks off with a Hangar Party, where exotic cars are on display, along with custom motorcycles, luxury boats, luxury motorhomes, and private jets. Twenty local restaurants provide the food, accompanied by wine tasting and entertainment.

The Saturday Night Grand Gala begins with dinner and a live auction. We have auctioned off items such as: being Roger Penske's guest at the 100th Anniversary of the Indianapolis 500, owning a one-of-a-kind wristwatch handcrafted for the event by Swiss watchmaker Ulysse Nardin, or spending a week on an island in Spain with five friends in a private villa. The most unique auction items we offer every year are some of the very first brand-new exotic cars delivered in America, such as Audi, Mercedes, and Ferrari sports cars.

During the evening, we present the annual Automotive Lifetime Achievement Award, which has been given to Roger Penske, Bobby Rahal, Mike Jackson, and Wayne Huizenga.

The gala entertainment provides the weekend's laughs. At the Yachting Rendezvous, the gala entertainment is always a top music performer. At the Concours, it's been a comedian. The first year, we brought in Jay Leno, who besides being a famous comedian is also a well-known car enthusiast and classic car restorer/collector. Leno returned for our fifth annual Concours event in 2011, where we presented him with the Lee Iococca Award, which recognizes outstanding classic car enthusiasts. Other comedians to grace our stage have included Bill Cosby, Dennis Miller, and Howie Mandel.

Then, of course, the main event comes Sunday. Vintage race cars and classic vehicles are displayed while a judging panel selects and awards the finest cars and motorcycles based on style and technical merit. There's also a pavilion full of fine wines and gourmet food from local restaurants.

Taken as a whole, the event is luxurious and classy. The most impressive part about it is that we have no paid producers, promoters, or staff. We rely on volunteers, so all of the money raised goes straight to the Boys & Girls Clubs of Broward County. In 2011, we set the record for the most amount of money ever raised for a charity at an auto event in the world by netting more than $3 million. We are setting a new standard for Concours d'Elegance events, as this has become an event to remember. The reason for its vast success is that it's making a difference in lives far beyond the people who attend.

In total, our events have raised more than $50 million for the Boys & Girls Clubs of Broward County, and in some years have raised as much as 50 percent of the money it takes to run the clubs each year. When we arrived in Broward in 1986, there were three clubs serving about 3,000 kids with a million-dollar annual budget. Ten years later, they hit the milestone of 10 clubs serving 10,000 kids. And today, it's one of the largest and fastest-growing Boys & Girls Clubs organizations in the United States, with an annual budget of $10 million, with 12 clubs serving 12,000 kids.

"That growth, which is phenomenal, is tied directly to Rick Case's skill and ability at marketing and creating, partnering with our staff and board to create events that appeal to specific donor's interests," Hughes says. "He's like an idea machine. He keeps coming up with new ideas and new events, and then he produces them himself."

In 1993, the Boys & Girls Clubs created an award in my honor called the Rick Case Pinnacle Award. It is given to a board member who follows my example of entrepreneurial innovation. In 1999, the Boys & Girls Clubs of America awarded me with its highest national honor, the Silver Medallion Award, for the successful fundraising events that I created.

The measurement of success for charity events isn't awards — it's the value that the money provides to the charity. The money we raise for the Boys & Girls Clubs enables it to reach more children with its resources, inspiring them to realize their full potential. Drugs and crime are a big problem in poor neighborhoods in South Florida, and anything we can do to keep kids off the streets after school and give them productive alternatives is worth more than any dollar amount. Success is measured in lives and futures changed for the better.

"He changed the face of the Boys & Girls Clubs of Broward County," Hughes says. "We were just a small, little organization, and as a result of his leadership and creative thinking, we became one of the largest in the country. There are more than 14,000 Boys & Girls Clubs, and we were always in the top 10. Sometimes, we were even in the top five, and in some categories — fundraising, for example — we were No. 1 in the country.

"That's the impact he had, and impact translates, for us, to saving kids' lives and changing kids' lives," Hughes says. "So you can look at all these fancy events and all these wealthy people, but what it all boils down to is helping these kids have a better life. Instead of us reaching maybe 2,000 or 3,000 kids a year, because of the success of the Boys & Girls Clubs in Broward, we're reaching 12,000 a year. And that's year after year. You can't put a price on how many lives have been changed for the better and generations changed. Rick's made a difference. We were lucky to have him."

First Yachting Rendezvous on Cat Cay, 1988

24th annual invitation of the Rendezvous 2011

Chairs — From left, Top Rendezvous supporters Rick Case, John and Jeanette Staluppi, Honorary Chair Donald Trump, Wayne Huizenga Jr., Fonda Huizenga, Doug and Linda Von Allmen, and Rita Case

Brochure promoting the 6th Annual Concours de Elegance event

Second year invitation for the Yachting Rendezvous

FROM THE BRIDGE by Jeff Hammond

CHARITY BALL AFLOAT

Take your boat to Cat Cay and benefit a worthy cause.

For years, charities have organized balls and other social events as fundraisers. Now there's an event for boat owners. Certainly the yachtsman's charity event of 1989 has to be the Second Annual Cat Cay Rendezvous which benefits the Fort Lauderdale Boys Club.

The idea is simple: In return for a donation, you and your yacht spend a few days on one of the most idyllic islands in the world, Cat Cay, located just 54 miles east of Fort Lauderdale and 12 miles south of Bimini. It all happens just a week after the Fort Lauderdale Boat Show, from November 2nd to the 5th.

One of the great drawing cards is the fact that Cat Cay is not a place you can normally visit without being a member. The island is privately owned by the Cat Cay Yacht Club, which is hosting the Boys Club event. Quite frankly there's no other place like it.

There are only 70 cottages and houses, all at the disposal of the club. Most are located right on the beach or just a few yards from the emerald-clear Bahamian waters. No cars or paved streets exist there. You get around with battery-powered golf carts or on foot. The only traffic noise to be heard is the gentle hum of the carts, whisking along the manicured walks toward the unspoiled and virtually uninhabited beaches.

Cat Cay is another world. None of the hustle of the U.S. and none of the bustle of Freeport. The loudest noises are rustling palm fronds along the beach, crashing surf, and wind whistling through the island's pines. In fact, there are only two or three phone lines on the whole island, none of them in any of the houses!

If you haven't been to the island in the last 18 months, you'll be surprised at how much it's changed. A new 115-slip marina has been built. The nine-hole golf course has been groomed to the hilt and beautified. In nearly every way, the island has been manicured into a little Bermuda.

Greg Norman (left) at the 1989 Boys Club Rendezvous.

As I've already noted, the Rendezvous, which is being sponsored by *Power And Motoryacht*, has a charitable aim. It benefits the Boys Club of Fort Lauderdale, part of a nation-wide organization dedicated to helping underprivileged city youths by involving them in sports and positive community activities. The Boys Club Of America instills in its members a feeling of self-worth and fosters confidence, pride, and integrity.

I cannot think of any organization better able to help eradicate one of our society's biggest problems. By showing young men that there are alternatives to drugs and crime, the Boys Clubs do our country a great service.

While federal, state, and local governments spend millions on programs that only perpetuate the plight of the inner-city poor, the Boys Clubs are working to give their members the self-confidence to climb out of the ghetto. Perhaps the Boys Clubs can't totally rid America of crime and drugs, but they *do* provide alternatives. Simply by being there, the clubs can give new direction to many kids and maybe even save some lives.

Growing up isn't easy in some places. For instance, the city of Fort Lauderdale is at once America's megayacht Mecca and an epicenter for the cocaine trade. (Imagine that entrepreneurial juxtaposition!) The drug business is a compelling force, in the presence of which even decent young men can succumb to negative peer pressure. The Boys Club is there to counter that pressure, to be a haven where kids can find purpose and conscience. Last year, more than 5,000 boys and girls made half a million visits to Fort Lauderdale Boys Clubs. That's some program!

A Long Weekend In Paradise

Rendezvous boats will arrive at the island on Thursday, November 2nd, clearing customs right at Cat Cay's marina. Nothing could be more convenient. Then, the fun begins. For three days, the island will be alive with activities from morning till night.

Last year, pro golfers Greg Norman and Raymond Floyd took on the yachtsmen in a friendly round, and tennis pro Butch Buchholz headlined a tournament on the tennis courts. Other events included an "Olympics" (...ever heard of a champagne glass relay?), a fishing tournament sponsored by Bertram, and Yamaha WaveRunner races.

This year's festivities will be at least as exciting. Even in the evenings, the fun will go on. As the sun sinks in the west, dinner will be followed by dancing and entertainment. One night will be devoted to an auction. Items scheduled to fall beneath the gavel this year include yachting necessities such as fuel and bottom paint jobs. Wives will be interested in jewelry and designer clothes that will be on the block.

Yet another evening will be reserved for "Casino Night." High rollers will get the chance to try their luck at the gaming tables and everyone will be a winner—if not the patrons, then the Boys Club.

What is really the most fun of all, however, is the camaraderie shared by a group of powerboat owners getting together to share stories and help out a worthy cause.

If you're going to the Fort Lauderdale Boat Show this year, plan to stay an extra few days and head over to Cat Cay. You're invited to join the fun at the PMY Cat Cay Rendezvous. Donations are $2,500 per boat of four people. Additional guests are $500 each and rooms are $750 per couple for all three nights. No boat is too small or too large to participate in this, the yachtsman's charity event of the year.

To reserve your slip in Cat Cay Marina, write David Hughes, Boys Club of Broward County, 2000 East Oakland Park Blvd., Suite 110, Fort Lauderdale, FL 33306. Or call (305) 561-2697. □

Article about the Boys and Girls Club Rendezvous, 1989

Rita and Rick Case being awarded the Boys & Girls Clubs of America's highest honor, the Silver Medallion, 1999

Pinnacle Award created in Rick's honor, 1993

Chapter 15

Lesson #15: No risk, no reward

Immediately after entering the U.S. market in 1986, Hyundai became the hottest-selling car in America. You couldn't keep Hyundais on the lot — at $4,995, they nearly sold themselves. Then in a downturn that happened almost as quickly, Hyundai was suddenly the nation's worst-performing brand in the early 1990s.

The car had picked up a bad image, a reputation that you only owned a Hyundai if you couldn't afford anything else. It had become the poor man's car, and a series of quality issues only made matters worse.

This low-class, low-quality image consumed Hyundai's brand. Despite a series of advertising campaigns aimed at boosting the car's image — including one that provided two years of free maintenance — Hyundai just couldn't shake the image of being a car that you didn't want to be seen in.

At that time, the main tools in Hyundai's artillery were giant rebates. That appealed to people known in the car business as "get-me-done customers," and if it did bring in business, it didn't last very long. Besides, when you give a $3,000 rebate on a $9,000 car, it really doesn't say much for the product.

Throughout the 1990s, Hyundai's executives tried every idea they could imagine to salvage the brand's U.S. image. All were futile attempts. Even Hyundai's own dealers gave up. Rather than come to the brand's aid, many of them began dropping the franchise as fast as they could. They gave excuses that the car was no longer in demand or that it required too much work to sell. The bottom line was that dealers were no longer making any money selling Hyundais and had lost faith in the brand.

By the mid-90s, we had three Hyundai stores — one each in Cleveland, Atlanta, and Fort Lauderdale. We were clearly in the minority because we believed in the brand despite its bad reputation. That's always been our style. We never gave up a franchise just because its reputation struggled. In this case, we stuck with the brand because we knew Hyundai was a great company. We knew they could be great again because Hyundai was the No. 1 selling car in Korea. We never wavered in our belief that it was going to recover in the U.S.

I was more than just a Hyundai dealer when all of this occurred. In 1996, when Hyundai's sales plummeted, I was a member of the national dealer council. We were the select group of dealers charged with pondering workable solutions to this problem. I took it upon myself to develop a visionary program aimed at putting the franchise back at the top of car buyers' shopping lists.

It wasn't like anybody from Hyundai called me up and said, "Rick, you develop it." But I had seen so many failed attempts at saving this brand that I recognized the only thing left to try was a crazy idea. And I've always been pretty good at coming up with crazy ideas that work.

Hyundai needed something big and bold, so that's just what I put together. My big idea to resuscitate Hyundai was a 10-year, 100,000-mile warranty. This would serve as the lifeline the brand needed by establishing confidence around the reliability issues — and, at the same time, it would be a newsmaker and a brand differentiator to turn attention back toward considering a Hyundai.

Coming up with the concept was the easy part. The hard part was selling the idea to the national dealer council and the factory, including the president of Hyundai from Korea. The dealer council and the factory were already skeptical that Hyundai could keep making money in the U.S., and on the surface, my idea seemed like it might cost the company additional money.

Undeterred, and with a turnaround plan in hand, I boarded a plane to California to present the proposal to the dealer council and the factory.

I found myself in a room of people who looked painfully uncomfortable. And why shouldn't they be? Here they were, stuck between what appeared to be two bad decisions: Throw in the towel completely and leave the U.S. market, or ante up another stack of chips and roll the dice again. But I was no longer that underestimated youth that the older dealers had called the "White Socks Kid." Now, I was a seasoned salesman who could sell anything — it just required an understanding of the market and a plan to capture it. I knew my idea was the right one, and I knew I could sell it to everyone in the room.

"You know," I began, "the biggest problem we have is that people are afraid of the quality of Hyundai. People don't want to be seen in this low-class car. In fact, they need an excuse to justify the Hyundai in their driveway when the neighbor asks, 'Oh, you bought a Hyundai?'"

And then I told the council my solution.

"I put together this 10-year, 100,000-mile warranty to put consumers' minds at ease. If a car comes with a warranty that long, it's got to be a good car. Why would we stand behind it for 10 years and 100,000 miles if it wasn't?

"This also gives them a response when neighbors ask why they bought a Hyundai. They can say, 'Well, my Hyundai has a 10-year, 100,000-mile warranty. What's the warranty on your Toyota? What's the warranty on your Ford? What's the warranty on your Chevy?'"

No one else in the industry offered a plan like this. It could be our competitive differentiator. With this plan, every Hyundai owner and dealer could articulate a reason that made sense to everybody else about why they should buy a Hyundai.

The quality issue was fixable. I'd been telling Hyundai for a long time that it needed to improve quality. But even if it had done so, Hyundai would have faced a bigger test: convincing the customer.

It takes years for consumers to test a claim like that and believe it. But with my plan in place, we had an instant solution. I told the council and factory we could convert customers easily by promising, "If you do have a problem, we're going to take care of you for 10 years or 100,000 miles." Nothing inspires immediate confidence like total commitment.

No other car company in the world offered a program like this. This idea would be instant differentiation. At that time, the top high-end luxury cars like Mercedes and BMW offered five-year, 50,000- or 60,000-mile warranties. The standard for most cars was three-year, 36,000-mile coverage.

My idea was to position Hyundai as higher quality than the competitors by showing that we had more confidence in our product. The warranty was really a way of saying, "Hyundai is a quality car, and we're willing to prove it." By firmly standing behind our cars for more years and more miles, we could get consumers to stand behind them, too. We wouldn't achieve this by tacking on a standard warranty. This could only be done with a commitment to quality far beyond what the competitors were willing to offer.

Why did it have to be 10 years then, and not eight? Well, because everything tied back to Hyundai's 10th anniversary in the country. I grounded the idea with a catchy "Big Ten Campaign," designing everything around the number 10. It was a 10-year, 100,000-mile warranty, a 10-day free trial money-back guarantee, 10 percent down, $110 per month, 10-minute financial approval, and 10-year free roadside assistance, all to celebrate Hyundai's 10th year in the United States. It was to remind people of the brand's history, to get them to say, "Hyundai has been in the market for 10 years, so it can't be all that bad. It has lasted this long."

Hyundai manufactured an affordable car, but because of the quality and image issues it faced, consumers were equating low cost with low quality. This was another facet of my approach, which I tagged my "Best Value Campaign." A smaller price tag obviously wasn't enough to make the brand appealing.

Sure, a Hyundai cost less than half the price of the average new car and even less than the average used car. But consumers could lease a Honda or a Toyota, cars that cost $5,000 more, for lower monthly payments. That's because Hyundai had the lowest residual value — or resale value of a car after two to five years of depreciation — of any car in the country, and Toyota and Honda had the highest. The company simply wasn't very competitive when it came to leasing.

With this new warranty, Hyundai could tout the higher value it provided, in addition to the low cost. This would help the company offer a more competitively priced product.

At the end of my presentation, the dealers liked it but the executives just nodded and gave the typical factory response: "We'll take a look at this and get back to you."

In honesty, the whole warranty idea terrified the Hyundai executives. They knew they didn't have a quality car to stand behind. Their initial reaction, according to Rick Lueders, who was Hyundai's national director of service at the time, was, "Oh my god, can we afford that?" They were certain that a 10-year, 100,000-mile warranty could financially decimate the company. They didn't even know how to begin calculating the amount of money they would have to pay out to cover the policies.

True to form, I didn't give up. I turned to the few believers I had won over to my side for help pushing the idea through. Because of their support, I knew I wasn't the only one who had faith in this plan.

For example, while this was all happening, Wayne Huizenga was laying the groundwork for a large network of car retailers that would become known as AutoNation. He already selected his chief marketing officer, and he asked me to acquaint that gentleman with the auto industry. That man was Tom Gruber, who was previously the vice president of international marketing for McDonald's before Huizenga lured him over to be chief marketing officer at Blockbuster Entertainment. When Huizenga sold Blockbuster, Gruber retired, and now it was my job to bring him out of retirement and into AutoNation. So the two of us flew to Atlanta for a big automobile convention where I showed him the ropes of the industry.

"On this trip, Rick was bouncing some ideas off of me," Gruber recalls. "At the time — this was October 1995 — Hyundai didn't have the best reputation for quality. As a dealer, Rick needed more national advertising and he needed more promotional activity and he needed some big ideas. And the company wasn't coming forth with any of those things. He wanted to know what I thought of his concept of guaranteeing the quality of Hyundai for 10 years or 100,000 miles.

"I thought about it awhile, and I said, 'If they could produce a quality car and really stand behind it for 10 years or 100,000 miles, you'd have one hell of a traffic builder.'"

Coming from a marketing genius who had worked with some of the world's most recognizable brands, this was a strong vote of confidence for my idea. For the remainder of the flight, Gruber helped me brainstorm advertising ideas to promote the concept.

"I thought about something that I had used very successfully with McDonald's in international markets where we didn't have the money to go on TV initially," he says. "In the early days when we didn't have a lot of money to advertise, we used outdoor billboard advertising, and we used it very successfully.

"I explained to Rick that you don't want to do what all the other dealers are doing and say a lot of words about who the dealer is and where he's located and so on. It's very simple:

Six words — no more — is the rule. Here's the line: 'Hyundai quality guaranteed, 10 years or 100,000 miles.' That's all you have to say. So that was our concept, and he got really excited about it because it was a darn good idea."

Having that kind of help and support from an experienced marketing professional was definitely the boost I needed to help my idea take flight. I needed all the support I could get.

Even Lueders, who was responsible for Hyundai warranties at that time, believed in my idea. He approached me after I first presented the idea and said, "I think that's a pretty good idea. Let me help you do some homework on it." Now I had an ally on the inside.

"Sometimes in corporate America, stepping out a little bit beyond the normal think tank is not always the smartest idea because everybody's looking around saying, 'What's the boss going to say? What are the Koreans going to think?'" Lueders says. "A lot of that in the car business is ego. When one of your dealers comes up with a great idea that the factory didn't think of, you don't want your boss to think you're a bonehead so you don't bring it forward. The tendency was to say, 'The Koreans didn't think about it, so it definitely was not a very good idea.'

"In fact, it was really a pretty good idea," he says. "My thing is: It really doesn't matter who comes up with the idea. Hyundai needed something at the time. I'm not taking a shot at Hyundai, the numbers speak for themselves — it was not only awful, it was god-awful at that point. We needed to do something out of the box. We needed to do something that nobody else was doing — something bold. I just remember Rick was pretty high on the idea — enthusiastic as well as prepared."

Lueders helped me drive the cause forward by providing a lot of statistics. He even performed a cost analysis based on Hyundai's current warranty costs. At that time, the warranty cost was something like 30 percent of the price of the car. A

Sonata, for example, sold for $12,000 and the warranty cost associated was about $2,600. At that rate, Lueders knew we would need someone to underwrite this new warranty before Hyundai would even consider picking it up.

That meant we needed to garner some real support and test this warranty out in action, not just theory. I would have to personally find an insurance company to provide the warranty on cars I sold. Starting in 1996, as a test run, Rick Case Hyundai in Florida announced it was selling cars with a 10-year, 100,000-mile warranty.

I knew in order for this idea to succeed, I couldn't do it alone. To truly work, this required proof of concept, and that wouldn't come from a single dealer in Florida, but rather a dealer group working together to advertise the warranty to the entire market. I needed to get other local dealers on board with my plan. So I went around and talked with all of the dealers in South Florida — from Miami to Fort Lauderdale to Palm Beach — and virtually every single one of them thought this was the greatest idea they had ever heard.

The dealers were easy to sell because they all wanted it. Why wouldn't they? Hyundai was going downhill fast, and they could use any help they could get to sell that car. If there was even the slimmest chance that they could reverse course, they were willing to hear it out. All it would cost them was about $200 extra per car to buy the insurance for the warranty — and that would actually eliminate their risk of giving the warranty. They were hooked.

I already had all of the advertising and promotions in place. I even found an insurance company in Ohio that was willing to underwrite the warranties — even if this Florida experiment ended up going national. We were ready to start selling cars that were backed for 10 years and 100,000 miles.

Shortly after the offer hit the streets, sales increased dramatically across all of the south Florida dealerships. At

Rick Case, in particular, Hyundai sales more than doubled. Meanwhile, national Hyundai sales stagnated. That definitely got their attention.

The head of Hyundai's national advertising agency was always in the dealer council meetings. The agency had nothing to advertise about Hyundai on a national scale because nothing had been going right. So this ad agency executive saw the warranty as a great opportunity. I asked for the agency's help to sell the idea. To see if it really resonated, the agency started assembling customer focus groups around the country.

Nobody from the factory showed up at these focus groups, and no other dealers participated — only me. It was just Hyundai's national advertising agency and I conducting these focus groups.

We asked customers, "Would you consider buying a Hyundai?"

The standard reply was something like, "No. No way."

Then we asked, "Would you consider a Hyundai if it came with a 10-year, 100,000-mile warranty?"

That changed the responses.

"Oh yeah," they said. "Yeah, we would buy a Hyundai if it came with that good of a warranty."

We presented the results from the South Florida 10-year, 100,000-mile warranty experiment and these customer focus groups, along with a solution to reinsure the exposure, to the factory. This should have given Hyundai all it needed in order to accurately calculate the potential cost of the warranty and realize what a good plan this was.

But Hyundai took much longer to sell than the customers and other dealers because its executives understood the reality of this program. It wasn't just about slapping an extra warranty on a product to boost consumer confidence. This meant Hyundai actually had to back up the warranty by producing a quality product that would live up to what the warranty promised.

"Nobody can say, 'I'm going to give you a $10,000 warranty and keep the warranty costs the same,'" Lueders says, recalling dreary statistics of how many transmissions failed in the first year and how many 'Check Engine' lights came on in the first few days after a Hyundai purchase back then. "Hyundai had to make some serious internal commitments in Korea, which was where all of the cars were built at that point. So they took a little time to get their act together."

This was the best possible thing that could have happened to Hyundai. It forced the company to drastically improve the quality of its cars rather than pay out thousands of dollars in warranty expenses. That, I think, is really why it took executives a couple of years to decide on the warranty — they had to decide to improve their product, not just approve the warranty. They knew that if they opted for the warranty without making any real manufacturing changes as well, the warranty could end up driving them out of business.

After making my case several times, I finally told the Korean president of Hyundai and the other factory executives, "Look, you have three choices: Either change your name, leave the country, or do the warranty."

The Koreans did not take my statement lightly. In fact, they didn't like it at all. But I've always been aggressive. I truly believed this idea would help the company, so I had to make it happen. Hyundai's national sales were bad and quickly getting worse. They were losing their best dealers and dealership locations. I could appeal to that truth because we were all painfully aware of it. But I was the only one who both admitted it and came up with a solution to fix it. Hyundai finally accepted the plan.

"The Korean management was nervous that they would break the bank," Lueders remembers. "But at some point in time, they said, 'Hey, if we don't do something, we're not going to have a bank. We're not going to have anything.'"

In September 1998, Hyundai Motor America President and CEO Finbarr O'Neill announced a new package called the Hyundai Advantage, which was marketed as "The Best Automotive Warranty in the Country." He announced that each new 1999 model would be covered by a five-year, 60,000-mile "bumper-to-bumper" limited warranty as well as a 10-year, 100,000-mile powertrain limited warranty. The package also extended our roadside assistance from three to five years with unlimited mileage.

"The warranty is our promise to every customer that Hyundai will provide a decade of dependability," O'Neill said.

The impact was immediate.

"I remember the first month we launched it," Lueders recalls. "We doubled our sales. It was out of the gate rocking and rolling immediately, so it worked. It definitely worked. By that time, I had become western regional manager, and I remember calling my counterpart in Chicago and laughing because business was so good, we weren't used to it."

Every year since introducing the warranty, Hyundai has gained market share. The number of Hyundais sold rocketed from 90,000 in 1998 to 164,000 in 1999, then to 244,000 in 2000 and more than 346,000 in 2001. Not coincidentally, the quality of Hyundai's car has improved every year, too. Today, you could call it the best car in the country. Hyundai now has the hottest and fastest-selling cars not only in the U.S. but also in the world — all because a warranty idea virtually saved the franchise in America.

"The warranty changed who Hyundai was and became part of us," Lueders says. "Now, it's a fabric of what the franchise really is. So it went from an out-of-the-box idea to what the company really stands for. They can't get rid of it. You think they like paying warranty costs under 100,000 miles? No way. But honestly, they will never be able to get rid of it."

The warranty was groundbreaking. Hyundai was the only car manufacturer to offer a warranty that extended beyond five years. It eliminated the industry's long-held assumption that a longer warranty put your company at higher risk. And because of this, longer warranties have become the cost of doing business as a new franchise — you automatically offer five-, six-, or seven-year warranties.

At Rick Case, we go one step further than that because we've committed to staying ahead of everyone else with innovation. Our dealerships double the factory warranty on every car we sell. For example, Honda has a five-year, 50,000-mile warranty, so we give it a 10-year, 100,000-mile warranty. Hyundai, Kia, and Mitsubishi offer a 10-year, 100,000-mile warranty, so we give customers a 20-year, 200,000-mile warranty — on every car, every day, at every dealership. In fact, we give at least a 10-year, 100,000-mile warranty on every car we sell, even if that's more than double the factory warranty.

Other dealers say, "That's such a huge risk. Look at how much you could lose. What if the transmission goes out at 198,000 miles?" We don't see it as a risk, but rather a well-thought-out analysis of how to create the result we want.

Other dealers theorize that if you give customers that long of a warranty, they will keep the car longer. That means customers won't come back any time soon to buy another car. But in practice, it doesn't work that way. Instead, the better you treat customers and the more you give them, the more they will like you and the faster they are going to come back to you. It's all about that wow factor; it's all about what it does for the customer.

Before we ever rolled out the double warranty at our dealerships, we calculated the monetary risk, and we weighed that against the reward of being able to tell customers, "If you buy a car from Rick Case, you're getting double the factory warranty." No other dealers do that, because they don't want the risk or the extra expense. So they don't get the reward, which comes from giving the customer real value.

Doubling warranties gives us a huge competitive advantage, especially during an economic downturn when consumers keep and maintain vehicles longer. This gives them a reason to keep doing business with Rick Case.

In 2011, Hyundai celebrated its 25th anniversary in the United States. At the convention, the company honored all of its original dealers. Only 13 of the 50 original Hyundai dealers stuck around through the brand's ups and downs. Two of those dealers were Rita and Rick Case in Fort Lauderdale and Atlanta. The mounting losses year after year after year, caused mostly by the negative image Hyundai had developed in the U.S., caused dealers to drop the brand. Being a Hyundai dealer hasn't always meant great times, but I chose to stand behind the franchise because my name was on the product, too, and I believed in that product — sometimes, I think, even more than the factory did.

THE PROBLEMS - THE SOLUTIONS

I. PROBLEMS

A. Perception of bad quality - Consumer wants to be able to trust that the vehicle will keep running.

B. It's not good to be seen in a Hyundai - Consumer wants the image to be that they made a smart choice and they drive a good car.

C. Not competitive on a monthly payment - a Consumer can buy or lease a Honda or Toyota costing $5,000 more for less per month.

II. SOLUTIONS

A. Marketing

1. The Big Ten Campaign
   a. 10th Anniversary
   b. 10 year 100,000 mile warranty
   c. 10 day money-back guarantee
   d. 10% down, $110 per month
   e. 10 minute finance approval
   f. 10 year free roadside assistance
   g. 110 days to make your first payment
   h. 10 Reasons to buy Hyundai
   i. 1 of 10 Best Cars in Lowest repair costs and Lowest preventive maintenance costs

2. The Best Value Campaign
   a. Less than 1/2 the price of the average new car
   b. Less than the price of the average used car
   c. Lowest repair costs - Jack Gillis' The Car Book
   d. Lowest preventive maintenance costs - Jack Gillis' The Car Book

3. Promoting the Big Ten and Best Value Campaign
   a. Billboard teaser program
   b. HMA spot TV
   c. HDAA TV
   d. All dealer advertising supported by coop
   e. Point of purchase materials for showroom and service drive
   f. Testimonials by past Honda and Toyota owners
   g. Third Party endorsements (magazine quotes)
   h. Spokesperson

B. Competitive Financing and Leasing

1. HMFC needs to be more aggressive and proactive

2. Need competitive payment for lease and balloon financing
   a. Higher residual
   b. Lower rate
   c. Both subvented by the factory

Rick Case presented this written plan at the original meeting to outline the 10 year 100,000 mile warranty as the solution for Hyundai

Chapter 16

Lesson #16: Adopt technology to build relationships

Many modern companies depend on new technologies to run their business. In our 50-year history, we've learned that people and personal relationships are the key to a successful business. I always tell my associates, "We're not in the car business. We're in the relationship business. If you sell a car, you sell one. If you build a relationship, you sell many." Technology cannot take the place of those personal relationships, but we have pioneered several ways to use technology as a tool for furthering those relationships and managing them as we grow.

Technology is an investment for the sake of both our customers and our associates. We've continued to maintain state-of-the-art computer systems and programs since the early days of our organization. We have been early adopters of things that seem basic today — computers, the Internet, customer databases, and e-mail marketing — because we're always looking for tools and ideas that help us better connect with our customers as well as our associates. Having up-to-date computers and software is one way of showing our associates that we care about giving them the tools they need in order to efficiently and effectively do their job — which is to treat our customers as we would our best friends.

As consumers move online with their questions and needs, the successful businesses will be the ones that position themselves as the solutions. When you have an attractive, informative website that shows up at the top of search results, you get people's attention. When they come inside your stores and you continue to meet all of their needs quickly and attentively, you keep their attention — and they become loyal customers instead of one-time, click-through shoppers. We use technology to further our relationships with our customers, building loyalty to the point that we create raving fans who don't just keep coming back to Rick Case — they tell all of their friends to come to Rick Case, too.

"Rick has changed with the times by doing things differently to keep up with the advent of the Internet and doing business online," Bob Bartholomew says. "Rick is probably the first one to make any of those changes because he realizes that those who don't change in this business will not succeed."

The first technology we employed in the early days of our business was the IBM punch card system, a forerunner to the computer that handled input, processing, and data storage by coding a stiff piece of paper with a pattern of holes. As outdated as it sounds, it was the best equipment in the early 1970s — and we had it.

As soon as computer technology was available, we jumped on it and switched our dealerships to a computer-based system. But there wasn't really an interconnected system for computers at that time. They were single-location systems. With Rick Case spread out in Cleveland, Akron, Columbus, and Cincinnati, we needed a way to connect all of our dealerships on a single platform.

To do this, we approached a company called Automated Data Processing (ADP) that offers payroll and other computer services for businesses and had started a division devoted to vehicle dealers. We asked them to help us set up a computer system connecting every Rick Case location.

Together with ADP, we developed a way to do it, point-to-point, using a phone line and a modem. ADP supplied the software and we found a vendor, a company called Infotron, which developed a device to connect computers to Rick Case Enterprises, our main office. The way it worked was with a dedicated phone line and modem. One or two computer terminals could be connected at the same time. For the early 1980s, this was very innovative for our industry because most dealers operated only one location. Therefore, there was no need to connect operations through phone lines. We were constantly developing ways to operate multiple locations miles apart in the most efficient and effective manner. With 14 motorcycle and car stores located from Cleveland to Cincinnati, with inventory consisting of hundreds of cars, motorcycles, mopeds, bicycles, with parts and service operations, it was critical that we could control the business daily with timely accurate information.

This was long before the average home had a phone line for the Internet, let alone routers where people could hook up multiple computers and network.

As we developed and fine-tuned this technology, controlling our business became easier, allowing for more growth. The computer system enabled us to expand into multiple locations while maintaining a central accounting operation. From a central office in Akron, which was connected to the rest of our dealerships by phone lines, we managed the accounting for all of the stores — including payroll, payables, cash management, and inventory.

With this technology in place, the only type of office position we needed at each dealership was a cashier. Everything else from the title registration to the paychecks was handled through this central office we called RCE — Rick Case Enterprises. Technology can be a great tool for efficient work force and asset management. It was the key to controlling and inspecting our fast rate of expansion.

Most companies today rely on technology for customer relationship management. We have learned that the best customer relationships begin face-to-face and involve a lot of personal interaction. That said, technology has assisted our philosophy of treating customers like our best friends by expanding and tracking our efforts.

In 1999, we started using a software product called Higher Gear to collect customer information, which captures everything with the swipe of a customer's driver's license and integrates it into our system. Each greeter station, consultant station, service advisor station, and sales desk has this capability to easily log every conversation and transaction we have with each customer. Every day, the system prints out a work schedule for every sales associate to plan for them who to follow up with, who to wish a happy birthday, and so on. The more customers you have, the more help you need keeping track of their information — and technology made it easier.

For several years, we worked on another computer-controlled innovation that we launched at all of our dealerships nationwide in 2002: our exclusive Rewards Card Program. Our idea was to give all customers a card they could use to accumulate points on every purchase they made, including service, parts, accessories, new and used cars, and even gasoline. Then they could redeem those points for discounts on purchases in all departments at any Rick Case dealership. We needed a system that could efficiently keep track of every transaction for each of our 200,000 customers — and counting. Still today, no other dealer in the country offers a Rewards Program like this for its customers.

Being able to track each customer's Rewards Points has become a vital part of our customer follow-up process. Every month, the system reminds associates to call all of their customers to tell them how many points they've accumulated. That gives us a reason to call and invite customers back into our dealerships to receive a gift or use their points toward a purchase.

In 2009, we switched from Higher Gear to a new Web-based technology vendor called Dealer Socket that developed a new e-commerce strategy for us. The goal was to expand our marketing reach and increase sales — all for a lower advertising cost. The plan implemented a lot of search engine marketing and e-mail campaigns.

Dealer Socket began by tracking the cost per sale by each of the different sources that direct customers to us. With information like that, you can make smarter decisions about your marketing budgets and methods. When we looked at this, we determined that we got less bang for our buck with traditional advertising methods. So we turned our focus to less expensive digital tools such as a new website, search engine marketing, and e-mail campaigns to increase awareness of Rick Case and, ultimately, to increase traffic to our showroom.

This data just illustrated the trend we were seeing all around us as consumers responded less to conventional media like radio, television, direct mail, and newspaper — and more to online advertising. They are using search engines to find information throughout the buying process, so you have to be online with the right information. Rick Case relies on technology partners to utilize search engine optimization so our site appears at the top of search results.

When you go to Google and type "Ft Lauderdale Honda," Rick Case is the top result — and that's just organic; that's not pay-per-click advertising. What that means is more traffic to our website, our phones, and our stores. Our best friend treatment takes it from there.

Another way we have attracted more quality traffic online at a lower cost is through e-mail marketing. It's a quick, easy, inexpensive tool to reach thousands of our customers and potential customers. It also makes it easy to segment our customer base if we only want to contact Accord owners about a new lease rate from Honda for that model. The best part about e-mail is the ability to measure all of the results. So if we send out an email that prompts customers to contact one of our dealerships, we can track who takes action and follow up with the ones who don't.

We had already collected customer information for 10 years through our Higher Gear software, so we had a large, qualified database. Even so, since we have started focusing on e-mail marketing more, we have seen our e-mail address capture rate go up to almost 100 percent.

This new e-commerce strategy makes it easy for us to manage and measure customer activity. In real numbers, this strategy reduced cost per sale from $340 to $210 per car while generating thousands of additional leads per month. This increased our Internet sales by more than 500 vehicles per month.

It didn't take us long to learn that the strategy had to be paired with the right people and processes in order to be successful. At first, we just turned Internet leads over to our sales associates. But at high-volume locations on busy weekends, we have so many customers physically coming into the dealership, and our associates are dealing with them face-to-face. That didn't leave time to respond to all of the online queries we started receiving.

We ended up adjusting our sales structure to accommodate the increased traffic this new e-commerce strategy drove in. Now, we have highly trained, dedicated Internet sales associates. Some of them are only responsible for responding to phone and Internet sales leads. An automated responder at our corporate headquarters monitors online activity for our e-commerce team. As soon as an e-mail inquiry is received through www.RickCase.com, the auto responder sends a confirmation note to the sender that someone will be back with them shortly. Then it signals our dedicated Internet sales associates to respond within the hour.

Relationships will always be at the core of the business at Rick Case, and we will always innovate new ways to nurture those relationships as times and technologies change. By working with partners to implement new technologies and strategies, Rick Case has kept up with the times and sustained our sales, promotions, and relationships through a digital age. This gives us an additional array of tools for communicating with associates and customers alike, for treating customers as our best friends, for making the sale, and for keeping our company running smoothly as we grow and expand.

Success Story

Case Study:

RickCase.com Uses New eCommerce Strategy to Double Sales

Dealership Increases Sales from 250 to 500+ in Just 9 Months - By John Zeiglar

With 15 dealerships in Ft. Lauderdale, Atlanta and Cleveland, Rick and Rita Case have led the Rick Case Automotive Group through tremendous growth in recent years. Founded in northeast Ohio in 1962, the group today is based in south Florida. Their line of cars include Acura, Honda, Hyundai, Mazda and Mitsubishi franchises as well as the new Rick Case Luxe Collection offering an exceptional selection of exotic pre-owned automobiles including Ferrari, Lamborghini, and Aston Martin, along with an outstanding selection of Mercedes-Benz, BMW, Lexus, Porsche and more.

With more than a half a million square feet, and over 1,500 new Hondas inside under showroom lights, Rick Case Honda in Ft. Lauderdale, Florida is the world's largest automotive complex. In March, 2002 (their first month and first year in operation) Rick Case Honda became the world's largest volume Honda dealer and broke all Honda sales volume records. Today, the Rick Case Automotive Group is enjoying tremendous growth in its eCommerce initiatives: doubling their Internet sales from 250 to more than 500 units per month while cutting their cost per sale from $340 per car to only $210.

How has the Rick Case Automotive Group achieved incremental sales and a boost in profitability during this growth period? Any high volume dealer knows that it takes more than a new facility and a lot of inventory to increase sales, profit and customer satisfaction. In fact, without the right, process, people and marketing strategy, a new facility and large inventory will only increase overhead and make it more difficult to turn a profit. One key to recent success at the Rick Case Automotive Group was their switch in technology and training vendors. The group put together a new eCommerce strategy and uses the power of search engine marketing and email campaigns to increase sales and lower ad costs.

The Right Strategy

Their new e-marketing strategy helped reduce cost per sale from $340 per car

Success Story

Success magazine story about Rick Case Auto Group's use of technology and state-of-the-art database management techniques, 2005

Chapter 17

Lesson #17: Support your community and earn their support

Davie, Florida, is a small town southwest of Fort Lauderdale. When we moved to the area, it still had cow pastures out near the Everglades. Building a dealership there was the furthest thing from our minds. Even though we did not have any dealerships Davie, Davie desperately needed a Boys & Girls Club. So Rita and I wanted to help make that happen.

Earl Morrall was a fellow member on the board of the Boys & Girls Clubs of Broward County who had previously served as mayor of Davie. Before he was the mayor, most people knew him as a quarterback for the 1972 Miami Dolphins, the only undefeated football team in NFL history. While he was mayor, the Dolphins Training Facility moved to Davie-based Nova Southeastern University.

As mayor, Morrall saw examples of juvenile crime and delinquency throughout town. He saw those as opportunities for the Boys & Girls Clubs to come to Davie and, as is its motto, "enable all young people, especially those in need, to reach their full potential as productive, caring, responsible citizens." The statistics show that juvenile crime decreases an average of 46 percent when you build a Boys & Girls Club. And Davie needed one.

Morrall wanted my help to raise the funds to make that happen. The first step was introducing me to Davie, which he did with a tour of the town. It didn't take long for me to notice that Davie is unique in Florida — especially South Florida — because it's definitely a western town. It's obvious in the Old West style of the buildings, and unmistakable at the McDonald's, where they have hitching posts outside for your horse.

By the time Morrall's tour stopped at the big rodeo grounds in town, bells were going off in my head. I knew how to bring the Boys & Girls Clubs to Davie. After one look at that town, as western as any town out West, I knew what kind of event would draw the most people here and raise the most money.

Right away, I said, "Well, this is a no-brainer. We're going to have a rodeo."

I don't think small, so I decided to do an event like the Calgary Stampede in Alberta, Canada, or Wyoming's Cheyenne Frontier Days — not just a rodeo, but a 10-day western festival with entertainment.

To open a new club, The Boys & Girls Clubs' philosophy is that there has to be assurances that the money would be there to operate it at a level high enough to fulfill its mission.

But first we had to raise the money to build the club. All it took was a phone call to Larry DeGeorge, a good friend of mine who I'd previously recruited to support the Boys & Girls Clubs. I asked him for $2 million to build a club in Davie. He committed to it, right then and there over the phone.

Next, what we needed was ongoing support from the community to fund the annual operation of the club, which can range from $400,000 to $800,000 a year. That meant we needed to engage the community because members of the community would be the ones really supporting the annual operating budget for the club. So the fundraiser had to be appropriate for the community. And in Davie, a classic car show just would not have been appropriate. By tailoring an event to the western town of Davie, I knew it would get the community involved and rally support.

At charity events, as in business, you have to think about ways to treat the customer as your best friend. You have to ask yourself: What does my customer want?

At an event, people want to have a good time. That meant thinking about the right entertainment, which in this case included western-themed games and activities and big-name country music entertainers like Waylon Jennings. We began to develop the Florida West Fair, an event modeled after the Calgary Stampede and the Cheyenne Frontier Days, the two biggest rodeo events in the world. I didn't know much about running a rodeo, so I got rodeo experts involved.

In 1995, Rita and I, along with David Hughes, went to the Calgary Stampede to conduct our background research on rodeo events. We met with organizers during the entire 10 days at the event. We asked questions like: "How did you set this up? How can we do it? Where do we begin? What do we need to know?"

They were very generous. They showed us how everything worked. We recognized that there was no need to reinvent the wheel, so we gathered advice from the pros and intended to debut this event with some second-hand experience.

"It wasn't just that Rick came up with the idea," Hughes says. "He was ready to invest his time and see how it works and make it work."

We also called on the help of some local event coordinators who could help us pull off something this big. First, I approached a good friend, Kaye Pearson, who developed the Fort Lauderdale International Boat Show and operated it through his promotion company. Pearson was already involved with some other charity events for the Boys & Girls Clubs. For our Yachting Rendezvous every year, he would load up a barge with extra docks from his boat shows and ships them to the Rendezvous in Miami for us to use. Once again, he volunteered to contribute some show materials for the West Fair, such as generators, tents, and almost everything else we needed to run the entire festival. His biggest contribution was volunteering his personal time and the time of his employees to help run the event.

Another local expert we sought out was Ron Bergeron, who is the ultimate local rodeo expert in South Florida. He is an iconic cowboy who competes in rodeos and lives on a 100-acre ranch. He is also known as a very successful developer who contracts roadwork and site development in the area through his company, Bergeron Land Development.

We invited Pearson, Bergeron, and several other community members to help put on the Florida West Fair. Years later, Bergeron still tells the story of that first meeting where we discussed the initial stages of the event.

"I'm sitting in this meeting, listening to this guy go on and on and on. I didn't know who this guy was, but I knew he had to be a car salesman," Bergeron says. "But he was so passionate about what he was doing that I couldn't resist getting involved."

After that meeting, I remember Bergeron coming up to me to say, "I'll help any way I can. I have room at my ranch where we can hold a party for the charity portion of the event."

"Well, how many people can you accommodate for a party?" I asked.

"Three or four hundred."

His ranch includes a 20-acre lake, two homes, and a huge pole barn perfect for events like this. So we added a segment to the West Fair called Ranch Roam where we sold exclusive tickets for a western party and dinner at Bergeron's Green Glades Ranch.

"We were never able to get Ron Bergeron before Rick came along," Hughes says. "We had met with him a couple of times, but we just couldn't quite click. Well, this rodeo thing finally rang a bell with him, and ultimately, the city named the town's rodeo arena in his honor because of the success we had at West Fair.

"That was the thing about Rick. He's kind of magnetic because he could pull people into his world and get them as excited as he is. That's how he got Bergeron involved, and then Bergeron got the local country radio station. Rick did a lot of advertising with them so he pulled them in, and then that opened the door to getting the high-end good country music singers and performers, which is the trademark of the event."

We phased out West Fair after about five years because Ranch Roam took on a life of its own.

Ranch Roam opens with western events for the whole family, from a western shoot-out and western music to old-time photos and Old West casino games. Silent auction items are on display this whole time, as we head into a seated dinner provided by a local restaurant and then a live auction. The auction items can be anything from the use of a horse for a year to a week at Bergeron's big ranch out in the Everglades to a Hawaiian vacation — even suite tickets to every event at the Florida Panthers' home arena for a year.

"This is not a black-tie event; it is a hoedown where people can get together, dressed western, and have fun," Bergeron says.

Bergeron got heavily involved in this event. He actually got so excited about it that he built his own private, covered rodeo arena at Green Glades Ranch just to be able to accommodate more people for Ranch Roam. The year he added the new arena, we filled it with more than 1,000 people — which was a record number of attendees for any event of the Boys & Girls Clubs at the time.

People come from the east side — Miami and Fort Lauderdale — dressed up in their cowboy and cowgirl outfits. We get everyone up and line dancing before the big performance of a well-known country-western musician.

Today, Ranch Roam, is in its 16th year and is making as much as $500,000 a year net profit, becoming one of the major annual fundraisers for the Boys & Girls Clubs of Broward County.

We raised enough money through all of these efforts to add a second Davie club in 2004, called the Rita and Rick Case Boys & Girls Club, in our honor. Juvenile crime went down 50 percent in the community after we built it, which doesn't only make the area safer but also saves the town money on crime prevention.

"We were in expansion mode because after we began to raise more money, it enabled us to start thinking about how we could reach more kids and reach out to more communities that need what we have to offer," Hughes says. "Rick is a true believer in what Boys & Girls Clubs do and how important it is to help these kids, who have so little chance to achieve and develop self-confidence, overcome what is often a very negative environment. That helped because when you have somebody like Rick, who's articulate and aggressive and is also a true believer, he can sell it. He was able to carry that through all of the events we developed."

Florida West Fair, 1996

Children from The Boys & Girls Clubs at the Florida West Fair with Rick Case (on horse)

Rick Case (announcing with his daughter Raquel) at the Florida West Fair, 1996

Rick and Rita received the key to the Town of Davie from Mayor Judy Paul in honor of their 20 years of support to the improvement of the community. Mayor Judy Paul, Sheldon McCartney, Rick, Rita and Sandra McCartney.

Rick Case getting into the western spirit at Florida West Fair

Rita and Rick Case (left) with Ali Waldman and Ron Bergeron (right) at Ranch Roam

Rick Case (left) with Waylon Jennings (right) at the Florida West Fair concert

Rick Case with Tanya Tucker at the inaugural Florida West Fair event

Rick Case (center) and Ron Bergeron (left) at Ranch Roam

Cattlemen's Club members at Ranch Roam

Chapter 18

Lesson #18: Stimulate passion to prepare youth for a career

In business, as well as in philanthropy, you don't always have to look too far for new ideas. The Yachting Rendezvous spurred the idea for the Biker's Ball and Biker's Bash. And then the Yachting Rendezvous sparked another idea.

Docking is very important to yacht owners because they want to show off their boats. They want to be in the front row so more people can admire their yachts. Within a few years of starting the event, we began to have problems because we couldn't fit everyone in the front row. There was no fair system, so people were getting upset because they wanted to be up front.

Every problem is just an opportunity in disguise. This docking problem, through my entrepreneurial eyes, was an opportunity for the Boys & Girls Clubs to make more money. If people wanted a dock in front, I thought, let's charge them for it. So we decided to have an auction for the first, second, and third choice of dock space, with people paying as much as $100,000 for one.

That opened up the floodgate of ideas as we began thinking of other ways to provide more opportunities for people to donate to the Boys & Girls Clubs all year long — while giving them more value in return. The next idea this sparked was the Admirals Club.

Yacht owners contribute $50,000 a year to the Boys & Girls Clubs, and in return, reap the benefits of membership in an exclusive Infinity Club — the first of several. Those benefits include invitations to restaurant openings and other special events — especially events that deal with yachting. While the admirals build camaraderie, they expand the club's philanthropic reach. It's a way to boost fundraising efforts beyond events and give people an additional opportunity to donate besides sponsorships and buying auction items.

"We got to a point where we were not only doing 20 or 25 $50,000 annual memberships every year," David Hughes says of the Admirals Club. "But we would get them to come up at the big black-tie dinner event at the end of the Rendezvous and make a commitment for five years. These guys would commit to long-term gifting because they liked the Boys & Girls Clubs and they liked Rick. They liked everything about it."

Other Infinity Clubs sprouted after that — the Big Wheels Club for contributors from Concours d'Elegance; The Leader of the Pack, which is tied to our motorcycle events; and the Cattleman's Club, which is attached to Ranch Roam. The Admirals Club is by far the most expensive to join; the others are either $5,000 or $10,000 a year. And 100 percent of all of those membership fees go to the Boys & Girls Clubs of Broward County.

After the Admirals Club was around for a couple of years, another idea popped up. By talking to some of the members who had yachts, I learned that the biggest problem they had was hiring trained and talented crewmembers.

I had just the solution for it — the thousands of kids in our Boys & Girls Clubs in the yachting capital of the world. Most of them — about 65 percent — wouldn't go to college after the clubs' support ended at age 18. The clubs offered scholarships and classes to prepare them for higher education, but it just wasn't in the cards for everyone. Most would immediately enter the work force.

So I thought, "Why don't we teach these kids vocational skills for careers in the industries that need workers?"

In doing so, we would prepare these kids for entry-level jobs straight out of high school, helping them develop successful futures. And, just as important, we'd contribute to the shortage of skilled workers in South Florida. It was another two-for-one benefit.

Rita and I, as well as several supporters, went around to local marine businesses, shipyards, and even the Fort Lauderdale International Boat Show, asking people what type of employees they needed most.

"We never have enough deck hands," people would say. "It's hard to find good people to clean and repair the boats. We always need cooks and stewardesses."

The statistics echoed the opportunity that their needs revealed, with the Marine Industry Association estimating that more than 109,000 marine-related jobs generated more than $8.8 billion in revenue — and filling all those positions effectively was often a challenge.

The $50,000 Admirals Club annual membership fees that went to the Boys & Girls Clubs would help build a vocational facility for the kids on the McFatter Vocational School campus near Nova Southeastern University. The 17,000-square-foot Admirals Club Marine Academy opened in 2006. The space included a woodworking shop, a kitchen, a fiberglass studio, and other labs to teach different technical skills that are often used in the marine field. We lined up industry experts to volunteer to teach different classes in the academy. The Admirals Boys & Girls Clubs Marine Program serves about 500 youths each year.

Then we went around to the different clubs in Broward County and told the children, "We're going to give you an opportunity to learn a career in the marine industry, whether you want to be a boat mechanic, a stewardess in the kitchen, a deckhand, or a woodworker. We're going to give you this opportunity — but first, you have to prove that you have the passion."

That's the biggest issue with these at-risk kids — often minorities from single-parent homes where nobody's there when they come after school. A lot of these kids don't have any ambition, any desire, or any passion in life. We wanted to inspire kids in our clubs to get excited about an opportunity and start thinking about their careers at a young age.

With the Marine Academy up and running, we moved onto the construction industry. We asked local construction firms like Moss & Associates, Miller Construction, and Stiles Corporation about the labor pool issues in their industry.

So we started offering vocational classes in construction; then aviation; and then motorcycle maintenance. We wanted to give the kids several options for finding a passion and a career. Today, the Career Exploratory Programs include culinary arts, media arts, motorcycle restoration, marine, construction, and aviation.

Most of these courses tie directly to one of our Infinity Clubs. The Admirals Club benefits the Marine Academy. The Generals Club benefits the construction industry. The Leader of the Pack supports motorcycle service. And so on. This just gives people another way to support the Boys & Girls Clubs.

These classes really fuel more opportunities for mutually beneficial giving. In the motorcycle class, for example, the students build a motorcycle every year that we auction off at the Biker's Bash to raise more funds for the Boys & Girls Clubs.

Wayne and Marti Huizenga receiving the Dream Makers award at the rendezvous (center, with award and flower bouquet).
From left, David and Kaye Hughes, Rick and Rita Case, Wayne and Marti Huizenga, Felix Sabates and the entertainer, Joe Piscopo.

Several of the Admirals at the Rendezvous

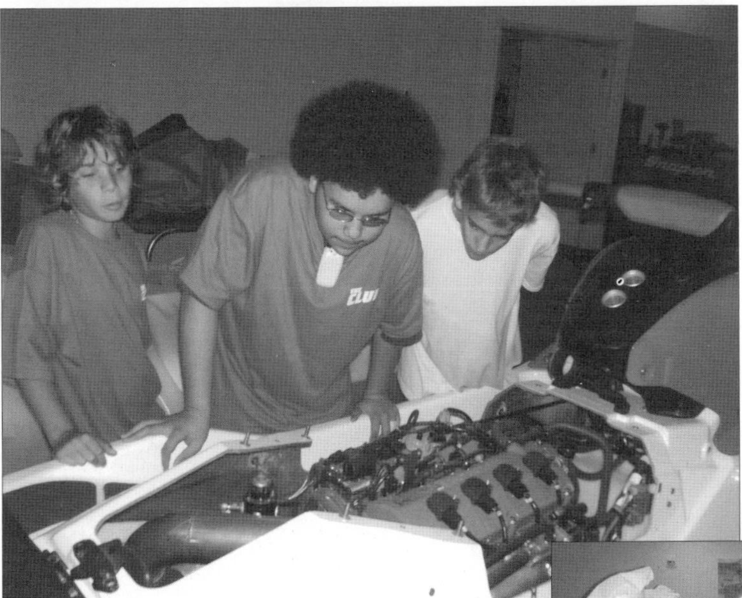

Admiral's Club boat engine training class

Culinary Class

Motorcycle training class

Construction woodworking class

Motorcycle built by The Boys & Girls Clubs' vocational program, which was auctioned off to support the club

Chapter 19

Lesson #19: Before you can be the biggest you have to be the best

In 2000, Honda announced its largest open point ever in the United States — in the fast-growing South Florida market. When a manufacturer identifies a prime location where it doesn't have a presence, that becomes an "open point," and the search for a new dealer begins.

All of the biggest dealers in the country wanted this open point because of the opportunity it represented. It would be the first new Honda dealership to open in South Florida in 18 years. Not surprisingly, the process was strenuous. Interested dealers had to submit very detailed applications in order to be considered. Honda received 106 of them.

I was passionate about this opportunity, so I prepared a presentation for Honda that was on par with the thorough presentation I gave Hyundai 15 years earlier to get the first Hyundai dealership. Your presentation and supporting material are very crucial when you're presenting deals like this. Even the most charming salesman can't make nearly the same impression speaking that he can with all kinds of pamphlets, pictures, renderings, and reports. The more you prepare, the more questions you can tackle confidently, and the better convinced your audience will be.

My closing for the presentation said, "Mr. Honda says, 'Give the dealership to Rick.' He has sold more Honda products than anyone in the history of American Honda." Fortunately, the Honda executives agreed and awarded us the new Honda franchise.

"There were more than a hundred other dealers vying for this point in Davie, Florida, and Rick put together such a tremendous presentation that he aced out the largest dealers in the nation," Bill Sander says. "There was a lot of competition for this, but Rick put together such a presentation to the factory — he had not only the artist renderings and the promise and everything like that, but he had a complete advertising campaign that he presented them with. So it wasn't just showing them the plan. He was showing them how we would succeed once the plan was in place."

When we broke ground for our Honda dealership in Davie in 2001, we had a promise to keep to the factory. We planned to make it the world's largest dealership in terms of sales. We didn't envision it as the world's largest physical dealership, but we quickly learned that once you start selling that many cars, you need room for all that inventory.

When we went to the city council to start the permitting process to build the dealership, all of the work we had done for the community of Davie over the past 10 years came back to us. The community was so receptive to our business that they changed the name of the street our dealership was on to Rick Case Honda Way. The mayor presented us with the new road sign at our grand opening on March 1, 2002, exactly 30 years after I opened my first Honda car dealership in Ohio. We didn't receive that honor just for having our business there — it was for the previous years of passion we put into improving the community without any business benefit. Before we even made our first sale from the new dealership, good things were already happening because we had given back without seeking anything in return.

After we used up all of the available land on this lot in Davie, we began to build upward. The following year, in September, we added a six-story building with more than half a million square feet to accommodate the 1,500 cars we keep inside. The first floor of this new building included an additional showroom, 40 express service bays, and a 50-bay collision center with nine paint booths. Our total investment in the dealership was now more than $33 million. That's how we ended up with the largest car dealership in the world.

There were a lot of innovative components to this dealership, but to me, those things were just common sense. We designed an air conditioning system in the service department so each technician could individually direct the air into their service bay. We did it because we wanted to keep the technicians comfortable so they weren't exhausted at the end of their shift.

The six-story parking garage with showroom lighting solved one of the biggest problems you have when selling cars in South Florida — the climate. Our customers can get out of the elements, whether it's the hot sun or driving rain, and enjoy shopping in a well-lit, covered area. When the customer selects a car in the inventory garage, the keys are delivered through the pneumatic tube system that winds throughout the dealership. All of this was designed with customer convenience in mind.

Right next to the express service center — which was the first in the area to be open on Sundays — you'll find our discount gas center. We installed eight pumps where our customers can buy gas wholesale with a swipe of their Rick Case Rewards Card. The gas center, like the free car wash, is not open to the public. Our customers can only access these with their Rewards Card.

There's a joke around town that this dealership really does have everything — and not just as it relates to Honda. Because I had acquired a lot of property in west Broward County, the clerk of courts called me one day to ask if I knew of a building nearby where he could rent or buy office space.

At that time, when you were on the west side of town, you had to go all the way downtown to pay speeding tickets, renew your driver's license, or get a marriage license. For the sake of convenience for our current customers — and the rest of the people in the western part of Broward County — I didn't hesitate with my answer. "As a matter of fact," I told Howard Forman, the clerk of the court of Broward County, "I have space. I'll let you come in rent-free, and I will also remodel it to fit your needs — at no cost to you."

The county clerk of courts office moved to our dealership in April 2004. Now, with "one-stop customer service," customers can renew their driver's license, pay speeding tickets, and even get a marriage license. The other thing we did was add a wedding chapel so after a couple received their license from the clerk of courts, they could go to the chapel next door and get married. We host between 20 and 25 weddings every month in our chapel.

These amenities are unique for a car dealership — as are the barbershop and the café that serves breakfast, lunch and, of course, Cuban coffee, which is a necessity in South Florida.

During local and national elections, we move all of the cars out of the lot and the showroom into the parking deck so we can transform the dealership into a voting precinct that serves 3,800 voters. We find that people want to volunteer to work at the polls here because we serve breakfast and lunch to the volunteers and supply snacks for the voters.

Why would I design all these extra benefits that don't contribute to our bottom line? Let's face it — I knew I wasn't going to make money on the discount gas center, and I sure don't make any money giving away free car washes. The plan was not to make money but to build customer loyalty. So that's why I designed all of these extra benefits — I wanted to get people programmed to keep coming back to Rick Case. To do that, you must offer customers something that nobody else dreams of offering. In our case, everyone needs gas every week, and most people get their cars washed once a week. Most dealerships don't cater to those needs. If we make it easy for customers to get these services from us, they'll keep coming back.

We also are open seven days a week at all our dealerships to ensure customer convenience. When you're building a business that's focused on the customer, you must do what is most convenient for the customer. Look at your business through your customers' eyes — they have jobs and they need to be able to get their cars serviced on a day when they're not at work. We know the last thing customers want to do is wait around for their car. That's why we aim to work within their hours, instead of the other way around.

Because the Davie dealership is the largest physical store we own, we had to think about creative ways to translate that atmosphere and convenience to our other locations in Ohio and Georgia. We recognized the space limitations — which means we don't have room in every dealership for a wedding chapel or gas station. We concluded that we needed to focus on the area that really set us apart — which is not a clerk of courts office, but the great service we deliver. So we focused on our Rewards Program and fine-tuning our ability to deliver great service everywhere that's consistent with our Davie dealership. Before you can worry about being the biggest, you have to focus on being the best.

When we opened the Davie dealership, Rita and I spent the first three months working on the floor, selling cars alongside our associates. That set the pace for them to follow. We became the largest Honda car dealer in the country our first month in business, in March 2002, by selling 734 Hondas — repeating our performance exactly 30 years earlier in 1972 when we first became the largest Honda car dealer in the country our first month in business.

A few months later, in August 2002, we sold even more cars and set a national sales record for Hondas sold out of one dealership in one month: 1,033. Not one of those was fleet; every one was retail. A year later, we broke that record again by selling 1,222 Hondas. This record still stands today. Our first full year in business, 2003, we became the largest volume Honda dealer in the country. That year, we also became the largest volume dealer for any brand sold in Florida, selling 7,294 new cars.

As usual, I couldn't be content with record-breaking sales. I started thinking about ways to make Rick Case Honda even more successful. Once again, I set my sights on a Honda motorcycle dealership. I guess I never lost the bug after we divested our 14 motorcycle stores in Ohio. But this time, it wasn't just about selling motorcycles to get cars.

Once again, it was about building customer loyalty and programming people to keep coming back. So this motorcycle dealership in Davie became much more — it became Rick Case Honda Powerhouse, where we sell every product Honda makes, from generators and lawnmowers to scooters and ATVs.

"We opened up a Honda motorcycle dealership so we could be everything Honda," as Sander puts it. "Rick was interested in the Honda motorcycles, yes, but it was the Rick Case brand he was building down here in South Florida. Everybody who bought a generator or a motorcycle was an opportunity to sell a car. They were now Rick Case customers."

By that point, our brand had become the main driver of our growth. People started to associate Rick Case with friendly customer service and one-stop shopping convenience. That's why I developed the motorcycle dealership — I wanted to be able to advertise that we are the world's largest full-line Honda dealer and that we sell everything Honda offers. That's a competitive advantage because no other dealer in Florida can say that.

"I've practically met everybody in this business, and the characteristics that uniquely define Rick are his boundless energy and entrepreneurialism," says Mike Jackson, chairman and CEO of AutoNation, the largest auto retailer in America. "He's a marketing genius. He just has a way of communicating that really resonates in the marketplace. It just seems to come to him naturally, and it's obvious that he loves the business and he's having fun. And you know, he'll probably do it forever.

"Of course, Rick is always selling, and I admire that from one salesman to another," Jackson says. "But part of his success in selling is he genuinely cares about the customer and he really thinks like the customer and treats the customer as he would like to be treated. Then when dealing with manufacturers and others, he's able to express a point of view for the customer and say, 'Hey, you know, you really need to do this, this, and this.' That's really where Rick comes from."

Our company is committed to treating our customers as we would our best friends in every facet of our business. We have learned that the more unique amenities and benefits you offer, the more reasons you give customers to return. But if you start building the world's biggest dealership without the cornerstone of customer service in place first, you'll be stuck with a big, empty dealership. Putting the customer first is what makes your business the best. And only when you're the best can you set your sights on being the biggest.

Rick Case Honda opened in 2002 as the largest dealership in the U.S. holds the all time national record for most Honda cars sold in a month, 1,222

Honda store team members with the celebration trophy for breaking the all time U.S. sales record — 1,222 new Honda's sold in one month, August 2003

The Town of Davie honored us by naming our street location Rick Case Honda Way at our grand opening

Rick Case Powerhouse celebrates setting the national record for the most new Honda motorcycles sold in a month, 614 in December 2005

Acura "World's Largest Dealer" award, 2002

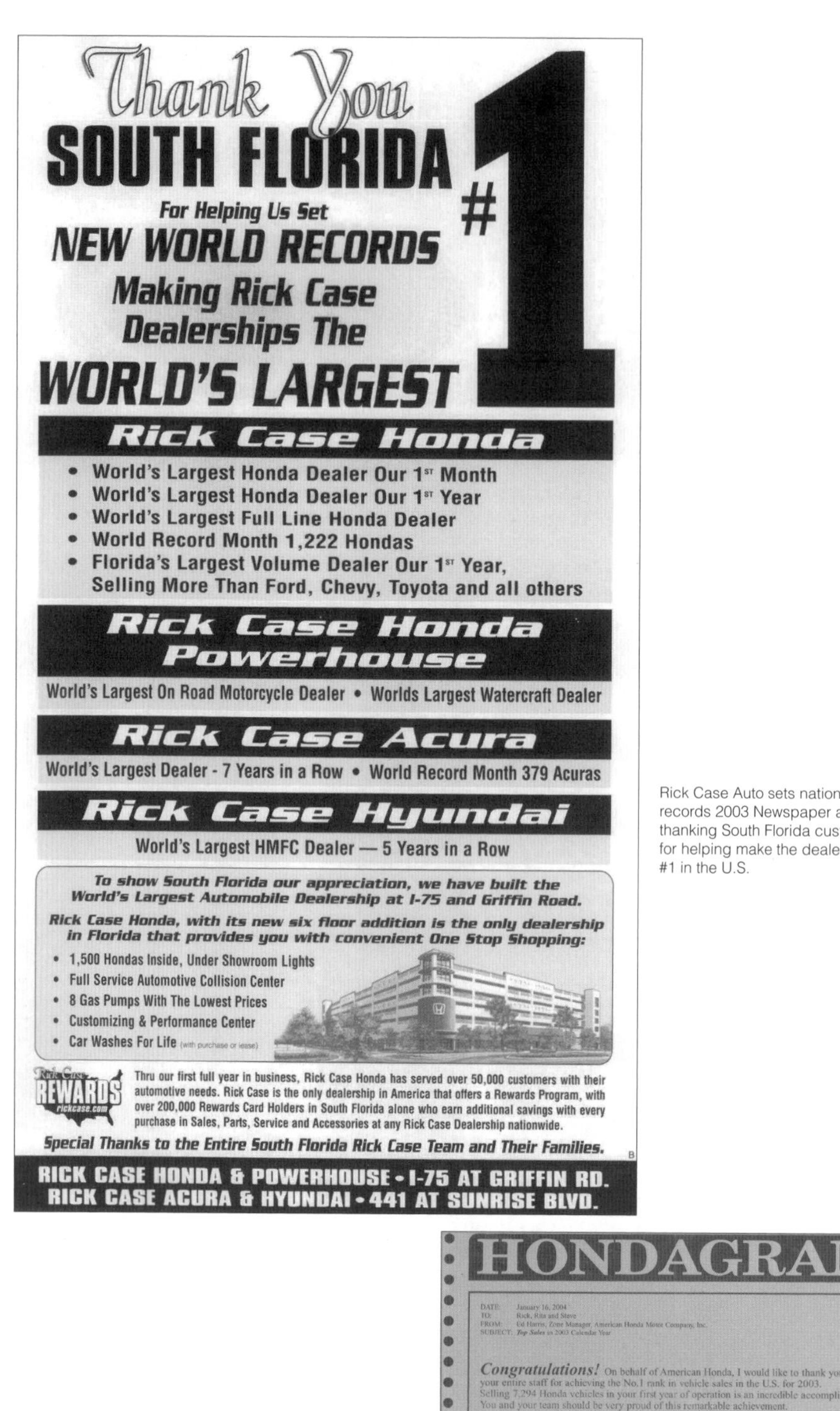

Rick Case Auto sets national records 2003 Newspaper ad thanking South Florida customers for helping make the dealerships #1 in the U.S.

Honda #1 store in 2003 nationally telegram from Honda — Hondagram of congratulations for being the top U.S. dealer, 2003

HONDAGRAM

DATE: January 16, 2004
TO: Rick, Rita and Steve
FROM: Ed Harris, Zone Manager, American Honda Motor Company, Inc.
SUBJECT: *Top Sales* in 2003 Calendar Year

Congratulations! On behalf of American Honda, I would like to thank you and your entire staff for achieving the No.1 rank in vehicle sales in the U.S. for 2003. Selling 7,294 Honda vehicles in your first year of operation is an incredible accomplishment. You and your team should be very proud of this remarkable achievement.

Your success is truly a reflection of your commitment to Honda and your customers. Congratulations, again, on a job well-done.

How about a sweet repeat in 2004?

Ed Harris
Zone Sales Manager
American Honda Motor Company, Inc.

HONDA

Chapter 20

Lesson #20: Make your passion contagious

People often ask how I'm able to do so much charity work in addition to running a record-breaking business. My answer is to repeat the old saying: If you want something done, give it to a busy person. When it comes to balancing business and philanthropy, that's very true.

A lot of people who want to help charities do so by giving money. That's easy if you have money. A lot of people can do that, as Rita and I do. But the hardest thing for any person to give — especially a busy person like an entrepreneurial business owner — is time. And it's not easy. It takes a conscious effort. It takes sacrifice to organize charity events in addition to running a business. You have to say, "I'm not going to do this other thing on my to-do list. I'm going to work on this event."

Because I'm accustomed to managing the busy schedule of a business owner, I know how to manage the busy schedule of planning and pulling off an event. It takes the same kind of commitment that I devote to my business. That means early mornings, late nights, and a lot of hours in between are spent on charity events.

"We got to a point where we were doing like 13 events a year," David Hughes says. "How can you be the world's largest Honda dealer and Acura dealer, and give all this time to a charity? I don't know how Rick and Rita did it, but it was inspirational. It would motivate us, because here's somebody that was willing to work so hard, and we're going to have to match that.

"He got up early, and I'd be in the office early, as well. So there would be a 5 o'clock phone call at the office — I knew it could only be him. We had a lot of conversations at 4:30, or 5:00 in the morning. That's just his nature."

It's really not that unbelievable. A lot of people keep full schedules for business, and they think that makes them too busy to make time for charity. But you have to think of it this way: Business owners actually come equipped with the skills it takes to start and run a charity event — drive, commitment, organization, and creativity. They just need share that focus and those skills with charities. Just as in business, a successful charity event comes from identifying a need, developing a creative strategy to meet the need, and getting people on board to bring the solution to bear.

Even though many entrepreneurs have the necessary experience to get involved in charity work, it's much easier for them to give money than to sacrifice the time. What sets the best entrepreneurs apart is that they have figured out how to use the traits that made them successful in business to get involved and help the community. And, most importantly, they make this a priority.

"You have donors and you have investors," says Brian Quail, CEO of the Boys & Girls Clubs of Broward County. "A donor is somebody who views your organization and says, 'That's really a noble cause, and I would like to support that with my money.' An investor in a nonprofit organization, though, like Rita and Rick Case, is a person who says, 'Not only am I going to contribute to you personally, but I want to understand your mission. I want to be a part of your mission.' When you have somebody who has that level of investment of not only their money but their time, their talent, and their passion — that longtime investor helps you to be a better organization."

Charity events, like a business, require a leader — a driving force to organize and execute. Events are more successful if you champion them the whole way through. You can't dream up an event and then turn it over to somebody else to bring to life, just as you can't hand over the keys to your business and take off. You have to see it all the way through. You've got to start it, run it, manage it, and open it. You need to lead the execution of an event just like you operate a business.

"People are always coming up with ideas," Hughes says. "Sometimes, people are idea people and not implementers. So they throw it in your lap and say, 'You do your best to make it happen.' But the unique thing about Rick is he'd come up with the ideas and he would implement. He would be there from start to finish. He'd be at every meeting. He would do the solicitations. He would partner with us. We'd make calls. We'd sell the event. He was there."

Here's my real secret to pulling off as many successful charity events as I have. As crucial as that leadership is, you have to realize that you can't pull off a big event alone, much like you can't run a successful, growing business on your own. That's the secret. You can't do any of these things by yourself, and you can't just assign it for others to do, either. You can't just come up with an idea and say, "All right, here's my idea. Do it." It will never happen.

The energy and enthusiasm you bring to the table is just as important as the behind-the-scenes leadership. It's that energy and enthusiasm that motivates others to get involved. When you can inspire other people, they will volunteer to pick up some of the workload because they want to get involved and help the cause.

"Rick is an asker," Quail says. "He makes it personal with other people, and he takes the time to tell people what the Boys & Girls Clubs do. He really knows the services that we're delivering, and he can say, 'Here's why I'm involved. Here's why I want you to join.' That's pretty powerful.

"Whether to sell cars or to tell a story about how you are helping kids in the community, Rick's marketing mind is brilliant. It's one in the same in terms of how he approaches people to say why they should give their hard-earned money to the Boys & Girls Clubs or why they should buy a car from the Rick Case Auto Group: He's an asker. If you've got something that you're very passionate about — and he's very passionate about what he does as a businessperson and he's very passionate about what he does as a philanthropist — you're not afraid to ask for the order."

In our case, we start asking for help in the early development phase of our events. The only way you can make a new idea immediately successful is by learning from the pros. We always conduct research on an idea before rolling out the event — by attending the Calgary Stampede and Cheyenne Frontier Days or the Pebble Beach Concours d'Elegance and the Meadowbrook Concours. We meet with the directors and the people who have experience putting on similar events. The due diligence step is just as important with charity events as it is when opening a new line of business. To get the best background research and advice, you need help from others who have been there.

I tell other event coordinators, "We're looking to you for your expertise and to find out what works. You're the experts. We want to be the best, so we need your help. How can we put this on the map? How can we become one of the best? Give us your ideas and your input."

For years, I've worked with Kerry Becker at the Boys & Girls Clubs to put on events. She began there as a receptionist and has worked her way up to director of corporate events. This is how she explains my approach:

"He always bounces it back," she says. "I love listening to Rick talk to the experts because he makes them feel so special and challenges them to get into it. He says, 'You're the expert. I'm just an old car salesman from Cleveland. I need your help.' It's like passing them ownership of what they're working on: 'Well, I'm going to rely on you for this. What do you think of this? How should we handle that?' And they eat it up. It's the funniest thing. They're like, 'Oh, you want our advice? No one's ever asked us our opinion.'"

In philanthropy, as in business, you need to get others involved because there are many moving parts and many different skill sets that go into a successful event. To me, that is really the definition of philanthropy. It's not just donating money — which is nice and does help. But it's really about helping those who can't help themselves by getting more fortunate people to donate their time and money at an event that is profitable as well as fun.

This, again, is where persistence removes resistance. You have to be so consistently and contagiously enthusiastic about the cause and the event that other people can't help but jump on board.

When you can excite the right high-profile people, they act as promoters and help draw in even more people. Just as I used performers like Evel Knievel and Russ Collins to attract people to Rick Case events in Ohio, I started using celebrities to add an extra wow factor to charity events I organized. For example, I had big dreams for what the Yachting Rendezvous would become. But in its first year, it was a new event and nobody knew what it was. I knew we could use some celebrity recognition, and that was all about connecting the dots: I knew there was a golf course at Cat Cay, and I knew who the popular golfers of the time were.

I told David Hughes my idea to bring in two famous golfers: Greg Norman, the hottest golfer on the tour, and Ray Floyd, who lived in Florida. I said, "Let's go get them."

Hughes asked if I knew them. I didn't. But that wasn't a deterrent. "We'll get them," I said. And we did.

I got them not just to play the course during the event but to also make some appearances at events beforehand to promote it. Their celebrity promotions alone helped attract more attention. Any time you involve people who are well known, like celebrities who people want to come see, you draw bigger crowds. It pays off to think big and to literally shoot for the stars.

"That's the way Rick thinks," Hughes says. "He doesn't think about, 'Well, why can't we do it?' He thinks, 'How can we do it?' And that became a part of our culture for the Boys & Girls Clubs of Broward County: Don't rule out anything. Identify who you could market an event to and how it would benefit the Boys & Girls Clubs financially."

Dealing with celebrities and affluent millionaires — let alone selling them on something — isn't a natural skill set for everyone. But my simple guideline of treating customers as you would your best friend applies here just as it does in business. In this case, the celebrity is your customer. You just have to think of the celebrity's needs and exceed them, the same way you would for your best friend.

"I was not used to dealing with millionaires or extremely wealthy CEOs 15 years ago," Becker says. "We had Jay Leno at our Concours event, and just watching Rick talk with Jay, you could feel the excitement of what he was doing. You could tell he thinks of our events like one of his babies, like it could be one of his dealerships. That's how much pride he has when he's talking about it. He takes ownership, so he makes the people feel like they're welcome, like they're appreciated. He made sure, when Jay arrived, he was there to meet him personally, make him feel like the celebrity he is. So the way he approaches celebrities is how he approaches everything: full-on, with 100 percent of his attention."

When you approach celebrities, or any high-profile personalities, you have to first treat them like your best friend. Then you've got to sell them on the cause by explaining what the charity is, what it's all about, and what it's trying to accomplish. A lot of charities speak for themselves — literally. They provide brochures and other materials to help you spread the word.

Next, you've got to sell celebrities on the event. When I approach people, for example, I illustrate how we run a first-class operation in the charity fundraisers we hold, and I prove our caliber of experience with examples of very high-end clientele.

As you're trying to gain support from celebrities and sponsors, the key to getting them on board is exuding pure passion. When you're visibly excited about both the cause and the event, it rubs off on others. You show them that it's going to be fun and that they're going to feel good about their contribution — and that makes it a win-win situation.

"He really cares about the kids," Becker says. "When he speaks about our mission in committee meetings or while working with sponsors, that passion is so evident, and you can see that it's not just words to him. He really cares about changing the lives of the kids that we serve, and you can feel it in his voice. And let's be honest, he's a car salesman, so he can sell anything. He can talk anybody into doing anything for our kids."

There's always something in it for the sponsor, and you have to make that clear to them. Sure, they're supporting a cause, and that feel-good sense of contributing is enough value for some.

Last spring, for example, Rita and I traveled to Switzerland to meet with Ulysse Nardin, one of the world's premiere high-end watch designers. Together, we created a one-of-a-kind exclusive watch just for members of our Admirals Club who have been with the club for at least five years. And we got Ulysse Nardin to donate all of those to us — a total value of more than half a million dollars. Anytime you hear of a luxury product manufacturer donating to a cause, it's impressive. Our admirals were amazed when they received these beautiful personalized watches at the 2011 Rendezvous Gala — and they were even more impressed when they found out they were all donated. It was definitely a win-win for everyone involved.

By the time we approached Ulysse Nardin, the Rendezvous had built a reputation over its 24-year history that helped make Ulysse Nardin comfortable with this huge investment in the event. When you're just starting out with a debut event, it usually requires more push to garner support. Because the idea is new, it carries a higher risk with it. Remember, persistence removes resistance.

After you make it through the first year of an event, people start to understand what to expect from it on an annual basis. Going forward, you don't have to work as hard to sell them on sponsorships. They have confidence now that it's going to be well managed, well attended, and successful.

"At one point in time for the Rendezvous, we had to put $100,000 deposit down to tie up Fisher Island," Hughes remembers. "Same thing with West Fair — to book these acts and to get the arena and the rodeo, we had to put half a million dollars at risk up front to get this to work. People might think that's pretty risky and that's dangerous for a charity. But Rick would sell it, and he would be there, and he would make it happen."

After a few successes, then you build confidence.

"We had board members who had been on the board from the very beginning back in 1965, and they were very conservative," Hughes says. "At first, when Rick talked to them, you could see there was a little hesitancy. They were smart to be hesitant because it was South Florida, where you learn real fast not to believe everything you hear. But after awhile, it was interesting to see the change. If Rick would come up with an idea, these same ones that were a little hesitant would say, 'Well, if Rick thinks it's OK, it's OK with me.'"

Once you start to build a reputation, it gets easier to attract support for your ideas and your events. Your reach expands, and people will start traveling further to participate in the event that they've been hearing about. Our Yachting

Rendezvous draws yacht owners from around the country, and it costs between $8,000 and $25,000 just to enter a boat. That means a lot of people come and give a lot of money to support a county where they don't reside. And they keep coming back because of the reputation and the camaraderie we've built.

When you focus on ways to benefit each customer — whether your customer is walking into your business or attending a charity event you organized — you won't only benefit the cause. You also ensure that there's something in it for everyone. By doing that, you make everyone feel special and important — like they're all integral in making the event a success. That creates relationships that transcend the event. When people feel important, they will want to work with you more. And, they'll want to keep giving, which creates sustainability for the nonprofits with which they're involved.

Jay Leno, Rita and Rick at the 2011 Concours d' Elegance Gala

Jay Leno, Rita and Rick, 2010

The Admirals

Rick, Rita and Steven Tyler at the Biker's Bash

Rick, Bill Cosby and Roger Penske

Wayne Huizenga, Al, Bobby, Al Jr. Unser, and Rick

Honda's President Award, the highest award recognition from Honda for outstanding customer service and dealership performance received 3 years in a row. Jim Roach, Senior Vice President, Parts & Service Division, Rick, Rita,Tetsuo Iwamura, President & CEO, American Honda Motor Co., Inc. and John Mandel, Executive Vice President, Automobile Sales, 2009

Chapter 21

Lesson #21: Adjust quickly to change

Whatever business you're in, changes will come that you can't control. What you can control is how you adjust to the change — which is not an option, but a requirement if you want to survive.

No entrepreneur can control the stock market, the economy, interest rates, or tight credit. But the smart entrepreneurs say, "I can't change what's happening, so I'll think about what I can do to make sure that those uncontrollable effects have minimal impact on this company's profitability, growth, stability, and employees."

Sometimes, you'll see an opportunity to advertise into the uncontrollable change to create business, like I have done with several creative promotions around rising gas prices. Other times, if there's not a way to market into it, then you have to make changes within the business to adjust to the change that is coming.

When Lehman Brothers crashed in the fall of 2008, my whole world changed. That was the one signal that told me a recession was evident. That was what tipped me off that I needed to act quickly. Some dealers didn't think it was a big deal, and they kept waiting around. But not me. I immediately called meetings with our top executives to discuss the situation and make plans.

Our reaction speed was crucial. We didn't wait to see what would happen, wondering how it might affect us; we just assumed that it would. We jumped on the warning signs and acted fast to adjust.

The first step to preparing for the downturn was looking for areas where we could make the most immediate cuts in our monthly expenses. The three areas where it made sense to cut back without severing any lifelines were inventory, advertising, and payroll. Immediately, we stopped buying inventory. We drastically reduced our advertising budget. And then we decided to initiate a round of layoffs.

Because we were discussing personnel moves, the next step was to assess our employee pool. We did this with the goal of keeping as many of our full-time associates as possible because they relied on us for benefits, health insurance, and stability. So we turned our attention to the part-time positions — porters, cashiers, phone operators, assistant office staff — where people worked less than 30 hours and didn't depend on our company for benefits.

Virtually every part-time position was eliminated, which accounted for about 20 percent of our 1,000-person work force. It was important that we acted fast and got the negatives out of the way before November, because you never want to make layoffs during the holiday season.

The remaining full-time associates were anxious. The air was rife with rumors about other dealerships laying off full-time employees and closing dealerships. Every time you opened the newspaper, all you read were stories about service companies cutting their work forces by big numbers. To soothe our associates' nerves, we went to them and explained the sacrifice we made with part-time positions to protect them.

"You will have to help us continue to provide quality service," we explained. "Fill in the void by working efficiently and communicating with each other to get all of the jobs done."

In a tight situation like that, you need to have fewer people doing more. You've got to keep smaller inventories. You've got to try to come up with better programs to increase your share of the business. That's the reason we thrived in 2009 when other dealers were losing money and going out of business. We had all of these unique programs that made a difference to the customer: discount gas, free car washes for life, and rewards programs.

The car industry is not recession-proof, by any means. But people will always need personal transportation. This proved out when the recession hit. People didn't stop buying cars. They just started buying less and paying less, switching to $20,000 economy cars instead of bigger $50,000 cars, and they held on to vehicles longer before buying a new one. Because I've always carried cars for the masses, not the elite, I had already prepared myself for this consumer shift.

For the most part, we stayed just as visible to our associates as we always had. Rita and I couldn't duck away and hide, but we couldn't start showing up every day at every dealership, either. Doing so would rouse rumors and cause panics. Rita and I kept making appearances at monthly kickoff meetings, where I would reassure associates by saying, "We're still a strong company. Rita and I have been through two other recessions in the early 1980s and the early 1990s, and we know how to survive these. We're a team. Don't be concerned about your position. Don't be concerned about the stability of the company. The best thing you can do is keep a smile on your face and keep listening to customers. They still need transportation, so we need to keep selling and servicing cars."

A strong positive approach is extremely crucial. I'm just naturally a positive thinker because I believe negativity gets in the way of achieving goals. During stressful times, it is critical that a leader remains positive in front of employees. A difficult economic situation causes a lot of anxiety for everyone, and they'll be looking to you for guidance.

"He exudes this positive aura," Bill Sander says. "I've never heard Rick utter a negative word — ever. It's always, 'How can we take advantage of this situation?' When the economic times were tough, his approach was always, 'We're strong. We're going to take advantage of this situation. Customers are out there buying cars, and they're going to buy from Rick Case because we'll treat them like our best friends.' He has never been afraid to go forward in the face of adversity. He knows that if you give up, you're done."

From the perspective of our associates, nothing changed in terms of how we ran the business during the downturn. A lot of dealerships later went into penny-pinching mode and cut employee luncheons, holiday parties, and other employee benefits. That is the worst reaction a company could possibly have during tough times.

Our associates heard rumors of that happening in the rest of the industry, so they were saying, "I'm sure Rick and Rita are going to cancel the holiday party. Or at least they'll move it out of the hotel ballroom and into the showroom."

To quell those rumors, we made an announcement in our October issue of Motorvations. We didn't directly address the rumors and say, "No change," or, "The rumors aren't true." We just ran the party dates and details on the front page as usual. We said, "Mark your calendar for our annual holiday party" and gave the location: The Signature Grand in Davie, the Beachwood Hilton in Cleveland, or the Marriott in Atlanta.

We didn't cut our holiday parties that year or any other year. In fact, we spent the same as past years on them, including door prizes from flat-screen TVs to iPhones and other popular gifts.

Because we reduced our marketing budget, we encouraged our associates to help pick up the void by directly reaching out to customers from our database. Phone calls and e-mails are practically free tools, and they help us personally connect with customers at a time when customers need direct contact from us. People were not thinking about buying a car, and we needed to remind them that this was the best time to get a great deal. It was a perfect marketing match to support the reduced advertising budget.

"In bad times, he makes the necessary adjustments and alterations to the business," Bob Bartholomew says. "If he has to cut back on budgets here and there, he does that. He's very intuitive in that area. But he'll also spend money to create money, where a lot of dealers in the bad times just roll over and say, 'We have to get through this.' Rick gets creative and drives the business."

The way you drive business when others are going out of business is by providing a value that differentiates your company. When times are tough and budgets are tight, it's critically important to invest in the areas that set you apart. For us, that meant continuing to fund Rewards Programs for our customers and benefits for our associates.

During this time, we kept associates motivated by giving them new ways to perform their jobs. And it worked. In 2009, even though we sold slightly fewer cars than the year before, we actually made more money.

Today, business is a lot better. In fact, business is better than it has ever been during our 50-year history. From 2009 to 2010, we grew our sales from $420 million to more than $564 million, and the percentage increase of our profits was even greater. We didn't add many people back that we laid off. We didn't increase our ad budget back up to where it was before the recession. We're still very cautious with our inventory, although the earthquake in Japan in March 2011 really cut our inventories more than we wanted. Obtaining inventory from the factory is becoming a more serious concern now than the local economy.

The recession taught us that we could do with less advertising, fewer people, and smaller inventory, yet still be successful. Instead of carrying a 60-day or 70-day supply of cars, we can get by on a 20-day or 30-day supply. Instead of costlier ad campaigns in newspapers, radio, and direct mail, we began focusing on Internet advertising and maintained our presence on network TV. The tough economic times helped us streamline to become even more efficient, preparing for the recovery.

We didn't always make money. During the first few months of the recession, we actually lost money for the first time in many years. But we certainly didn't lose nearly as much as we would have if we waited to see what would happen. The key was that we acted fast, and we could act fast because we were so close to the pulse of what was going on around us.

As entrepreneurs, you always have to stay aware of what's happening in your field — and beyond. The car business is usually the first to enter into a recession and the first to come out. But I had to have my eyes on the banking and real estate industries to see the indicators of this one coming. People who don't pay attention to what's coming around the corner are the ones who get in trouble. You have to be on your game, not just within your industry but also within the local, national, and global economy.

When you know what's happening around you, only then can you predict what's coming next and successfully stay ahead of the curve. You have to have the insight to know what's happening, and you have to be prepared to react to it quickly. With those two keys, entrepreneurs make the uncontrollable a little easier to control.

Rick Case Automotive Group Continues To Out Perform The Industry And 2008

While Industry Sales are down 27% from last June and 35% YTD. Nationally Hyundai Sales are down 24% from last June and 11% YTD, **while all Rick Case Hyundai sales up 14% over last June and 12% YTD!**

Rick Case Hyundai Plantation sales are up 23% over last June and used car sales up 156% over last June and up 26% YTD. **Rick Case Hyundai Davie** new sales up 15% YTD and used up 82% over last June. **Rick Case Hyundai Cleveland** sales are up 44% over last June and 34% YTD. **Rick Case Hyundai Bedford** sales are up 38% over last June and up 16% YTD and Parts were up 23% over last June. **Rick Case Hyundai Roswell** sales are up 20% YTD and used sales are up 18% over May and Service is up 51% over last June and 21% YTD and Parts up 58% over last June and 38% YTD. **Rick Case Hyundai Duluth** sales are up 38% over last June and 5% YTD and used sales are up 64% over May.

Nationally Acura sales are down 34% compared to last June and 34% YTD, while **Rick Case Acura sales are up 10% over last June and 2% YTD** and Rick Case Acura is the only dealer in the top 50 that sales are up over last year. Rick Case Acura is still #1 in the SE Zone for the Month and YTD. Plus Acura used sales are up 104% over last June and 24% YTD and parts and service are up 14% YTD.

Rick Case Honda has been #1 in the Southeast US Zone in new car sales every month this year and YTD. While Honda national was only up 2%, **Rick Case Honda sales were up 13%** over last month and Rick Case Honda outsold the neighboring Toyota dealer, Maroone by 165% in June and over double YTD. Honda for 3rd month in a row outsold Toyota in South Florida again in June and YTD. Rick Case Honda Service was up 24% over last June. **Rick Case Honda Cleveland** used is up 37% over May and service is up 42% over last June and 24% YTD.

Rick Case Cycles service was up 12% over May and parts was up 24%.

Audi sales new are up 46% over May and used are up 100% over last June and 32% YTD.

Hyundai The Shinning Star In A Gloomy Year

Hyundai was the 6th best selling brand in the country in June passing Dodge for the first time. Only Ford, Toyota, Chevy and Nissan sold more. For the first half of 2009 Hyundai market share increased dramatically from 3.1% to 4.3%.

HYUNDAI J.D. POWER AND ASSOCIATES IQS AWARD WINNER

Hyundai has once again accomplished an outstanding quality achievement, with the J.D Power and Associates Initial Quality Survey (IQS3) naming Hyundai the Number One Non-Premium auto maker for quality. Hyundai finished first ahead of Toyota, Honda Nissan and all other non-premium nameplates and fourth over all manufacturers behind only Lexus, Porsche and Cadillac. This is the second time in four years that Hyundai has beaten all other non-premium nameplates.

Hyundai #1 in Non-Premium Nameplate, beating Toyota, Honda and Nissan
Genesis #1 "All New/Re-Designed Model" and ties the Lexus brand
Elantra is also a "Top 10 Industry Leading Model" (out of 245 models)
Hyundai #4 in Industry, behind only Lexus, Porsche and Cadillac
Elantra #1 in the Compact Car Segment, beating Prius, Civic and Corolla
Accent #2 in the Sub-Compact Car Segment (missing #1 by just one point)

HYUNDAI ASSURANCE GAS LOCK PROGRAM

July 1st Hyundai kicked off its **Summer Sales Event** which offers customers a new incentive – **a locked in price for gasoline at $1.49, for an entire year.** Hyundai will provide new buyers with a Hyundai Assurance Gas Lock card, which must be linked to a valid Visa, MasterCard, American Express or Discovery credit or check card. A unique pin will be given to the customer, which will be used at the pump to purchase gas and secure the $1.49 price for regular unleaded fuel regardless of the listed gas price at the station. The program is available at more than 93 percent of retail gas locations nationwide, including Amoco, Chevron, BP, Shell, Exxon Mobile, Sunoco, K and more. Now through August 31, 2009 when customers purchase or lease a new Hyundai they receive the $1.49 gas price protection on Sonata, Santa Fe, Elantra and Accent (excludes the base Accent); plus the Hyundai Assurance 1-year vehicle no-cost return program which allows them to return their vehicle if they lose their job.

Rick Case Beats All Other Dealers To The Punch Again!

Rick Case is one of the first dealers helping consumers take advantage of the new government program Cash for Clunkers, officially know as C.A.R.S., and started selling cars as of July 1st. All Rick Case dealerships are making the program rebates available to all who qualify plus matching the rebate with savings up to $9,000 on select models. Utilizing a huge direct mail campaign with e-mail blasts, TV, radio and newspaper advertising in all markets, Rick Case has already sold numerous new vehicles under the C.A.R.S. program. And as of July 10th 7% of all Hyundais sold nationally were on the C.A.R.S. program. Please tell all your family, friends, and neighbors to check the rickcase.com website to see if their car qualifies for the government C.A.R.S. program trade in rebate of $3,500 or $4,500.

Rick Case Celebrates Independence Day

Rick Case was a proud sponsor of several local Independence Day Celebrations! The City of Weston had their annual parade which included Rick Case motorcycles, scooters and smart cars while the Town of Davie offered the full line of Rick Case products, Acura, Hyundai, smart and Honda cars, cycles and personal watercraft at their fireworks extravaganza! Senator Nan Rich (photo)

RICK CASE ACURA • FT. LAUDERDALE
SE ZONE'S LARGEST DEALER
June 2009 & YTD
Congratulations **Marc Riley** & his team!

RICK CASE HONDA • DAVIE
SE ZONE'S LARGEST DEALER
June 2009 & YTD
Congratulations **Richard Bustillo** & his team!

RICK CASE HONDA POWERHOUSE • DAVIE
SE ZONE'S LARGEST DEALER
June 2009 & YTD
Congratulations **Rusty Johnson** & his team!

Motorvations newsletter July 2009 how Rick Case Auto Group dramatically outpaced the industry for the year.

Chapter 22

Lesson #22: You can overcome any obstacle you believe you can

When Daimler AG (Mercedes Benz) introduced its "smart car" to America in 2007, the tiny European auto seemed to have a lot in common with other brands Rick Case carried. Like most cars we sold, smart cars were very affordable. Models starting at $12,000.

Also, like several cars I had pioneered before, customer perceptions of the smart car were often tinged with mockery. It was basically the modern, eco-friendly version of the Honda 600, designed for urban settings and short commutes. People called the squat 8-foot 8-inch car a "glorified golf cart."

The compact car that smart came out with, named the ForTwo, looked much different than anything to hit the streets in years. Given my experience and success pioneering unique concepts like this, I couldn't wait to get my hands on it. I knew we could sell a lot of them.

Mercedes selected Penske Automotive as the exclusive smart car distributor to set up its network in North America. Penske received thousands of applications for the smart dealership, and then considered about 500 serious contenders for the 75 total dealerships that would open in the United States. The franchise was only supposed to go to Mercedes dealers, but we sold Penske on the fact that we were the most experienced dealers when it came to pioneering new small car brands like this.

Though we were up against several Mercedes dealers in Broward County, Penske awarded us with the smart car dealership. We spent $2 million to build the first standalone smart dealership in the U.S. to create Rick Case smart Center Weston.

The sales process at a smart dealership was much different than most, and that was a direct impact of branding in the digital age. In 2007, smart launched a website where customers could reserve a car for $99. Penske Automotive made the first 1,000 online reservations very detailed. The system gave smart an early understanding of what models and features buyers wanted so dealers would be prepared when they began delivering cars in January 2008.

That reservation system was a great tool. So when customers walk into a smart dealership, they can place their order themselves on a computer. Dealerships provide product information, test drives, display models, and service, but inventory and orders all go through the factory website.

That meant that sometimes customers had to wait months for their new smart car to ship. So to offer smart customers the Rick Case experience, I gave them access to other fuel-efficient used cars from my adjacent lot while they waited to receive their new smart car.

With that service, in addition to our other unique rewards and our commitment to treat every customer as our best friend, we became the No. 1 volume smart car dealer in the country.

"Rick and Rita intend to be No. 1 at everything they start, and they succeed time and time again," says Roger Penske, chairman of Penske Corp. "As a team, and individually, you couldn't ask for better business partners of competitors. First class all the way."

Then, in 2011, Mercedes Benz decided to distribute smart cars themselves and bought the distributorship back from Penske. Mercedes went back to its initial rule that only Mercedes dealers could carry smart cars — which meant taking our franchise away.

But we didn't resign to panicking: "Oh my gosh, what are we going to do?" We immediately said, "What can we use this facility for? What opportunities are available right now?"

We knew Fiat was coming back to the country, so we started writing letters and making phone calls to Chrysler, saying we had the perfect facility for a Fiat dealership. Many others would not have considered this an opportunity — just another losing battle. That's because when Fiat bought Chrysler, bringing Fiat back into the country in March 2011, Fiat said it would only give its cars to Chrysler dealerships.

Of course, that didn't stop me from requesting one, even after Chrysler said, "Sorry, we've already committed to the dealer five miles up the street from you."

I said, "Come on, you've got to have me. I'm the best guy in the country at pioneering a new small car."

That is the biggest thing I've done to secure franchise acquisitions and open points throughout my career — to convincing the factory that I was the perfect dealer for its brand. Of course, it made it easier having the track record to back it up.

"When it comes to acquiring franchises, we present the best location and marketing, and we have a great reputation for selling in volume and taking care of our customers. This is what every manufacturer is looking for," the Rick Case Auto Group President Jack "JJ" Jackintelle says.

Of course, we illustrated why we're the best option through all of the record-breaking statistics, awards, and unique services we offer. And it helped tremendously that I still held the record in America for the most Fiats ever sold in one month. The last time I broke a record for this franchise was in February 1974, a cold, short month in Cuyahoga Falls, Ohio, when we sold 167 Fiats. That record still stands today, as Fiat left the country in 1984.

I sealed the deal with my signature claim: "Give me the Fiat dealership," I said, like I had told Honda 40 years ago in Ohio and again 10 years ago in Florida, "and I'll be your biggest volume dealer in the country my first month in business."

Fiat awarded me the dealership, and on May 31, 2011, Rick Case smart Center Weston closed its doors and began a total renovation of the exterior and interior to meet Fiat design requirements. In less than a month, on June 28, we were open for business. Other dealers who got their Fiat dealerships six months earlier were still attempting to complete the building or remodeling of their dealerships.

The people at Chrysler told me, "We've never seen someone like you. We've got to push all the other dealers to get stuff done, but we can't even keep up with you."

This wasn't the first time we made such a quick turnaround to acquire a franchise. Just a few years earlier, in March 2007, we put together a proposal — in both English and German — for the president of Audi because we wanted to open an Audi dealership in the Atlanta area. Within a month after Audi awarded us the franchise, we opened.

Before you open a new franchise, there's a lot of work to be done in terms of rebuilding or remodeling a dealership to meet the image requirements of the brand — which is an entire process of dealing with contractors and city officials to get building permits and approvals. The way we keep things on pace is by first setting a date for a grand opening event. That acts as a deadline to keep the contractors under pressure to finish on time. This is where an impatient desire to be the first can actually be a positive motivator.

It was crucial for us that we opened this new Fiat dealership before any other Fiat dealer in South Florida. However, the speed of this particular opening did present several challenges.

"There was no reason why we'd be the largest dealership in the country our first month in business," says Jackintelle. "We'd been open less than anybody else, and we were competing against Beverly Hills Fiat and the Fiat in Austin, Texas — both were well-established and they already had a customer base. We didn't even have the occupancy permit until the day we opened. Without Rick putting it out there as a challenge, I would have never set my expectations that high."

With those challenges surrounding us, it was more important than ever to raise the bar and rally our team around the goal. High aspirations really push you to challenge yourself and reach further. When the situation looks treacherous, the solution is actually setting your sights above the problems.

I called Jackintelle one day and said, "When we open Fiat, I want to be the largest dealer in the United States our first month of business. Give me your word that we'll be No. 1." And he committed to it.

That commitment has to trickle all the way down in order to truly get everyone on board with the goal. That meant Jackintelle had to get my daughter Raquel, who is the Studio Director (General Manager) of the Fiat dealership in Davie, just as fired up as we were. For a Case woman who was raised by two of the most passionate auto dealers around, that wasn't too hard to do.

It's all about passion, intensity, hard work, and drive, drive, drive. I just had that burning desire that we were going to be No. 1, and because of that, I sparked the same drive in others. If you're passionate when you rally your people around a goal — even one that seems out of reach — you will excite them about the prospect of being the best. Being an industry leader never comes easy; you have to push yourself and challenge your people to achieve it. We convinced our team that we were going to be the No. 1 Fiat dealer in the country by setting their sights beyond Fiat — to the future franchises that this success could help us earn.

"There are other dealerships we want to get next," I told them. "The best way for us to get those dealerships is to show these other factories that we became a Fiat dealer when they were only awarding it to Chrysler dealers. And not only that — in the first month of business, we became the largest in the country."

Whether you realize it or not, you always see people and situations in a certain way, and what you see is generally what you get. Throughout my life, I have realized that the more positive you are about your environment, the better everything seems. No matter how doomed a situation appears, you can always replace the negative with positive. That attitude becomes contagious, especially when you're in a leadership position.

When you walk into someone's office and say, "We're going to accomplish this," at first that person might think, "No, we can't do that." But if you keep turning the negatives around and showing people you believe it will happen, that rubs off. They'll start to believe they can do it, too.

And sure enough, in July — our first month in business — we became the largest Fiat dealer in the country and we set a new record for the most Fiats sold in one month in the United States. Since they returned, my 1974 record still stands as the most Fiats ever sold, though Raquel has made it clear she plans to break my record soon.

"One of the most important things Rick has taught me is that there's really nothing we can't get done. If you really want to get it done, you can get it done," Jackintelle says. "He has definitely raised the bar on what I think. Of course, with every store we open up now, we want to outsell everybody in the country. Things can get done if you really want them to get done."

Jackintelle says one of his favorite stories to illustrate this philosophy of "You can achieve if you believe," comes from my ability to literally move walls to make things happen. This is how he tells it:

"We own dealerships on Interstate 90 in Cleveland, where the state decided to put up a huge concrete sound barrier/ privacy wall between the freeway and the residents along the freeway. This wall goes on for miles. Well, our dealership happens to be along the freeway. You drive down the street and you don't know we exist.

"So Rick flies to Cleveland for the holiday party, and he drives to the store and realizes there's a 20-foot wall there now. He told his general manager, 'Why did you let them put up the wall?' Of course, the manager looked at him like he had four eyes and said, 'The state put the wall up. There wasn't anything I could do about it.'

"Rick said, 'I'll show you what you can do.' And you know, within the year, the wall was taken down from that section. Still to this day, from the section where our dealerships start to the section where our dealerships stop, it's gone. They are the only dealerships you can see from I-90. He was able to do that through lobbying the state, explaining the negative effect on our business, and paying to take the wall down. Every time I go to Cleveland, I get motivated when I drive by. It looks like a tooth missing out of the mouth."

It just goes to show that if you want something badly enough and you believe that it will happen, you can make it happen. You can even move walls — literally — and sometimes that's what you have to do in order to reach your goals and be the best.

"The lessons learned in life with Rick are simple: work hard and enjoy life," Bob Bartholomew says. "Rick has proven the old American dream — you can get whatever you want if you work hard enough for it. He started in the business selling a car on his parents' front lawn. Look where he's at today with 15 dealerships, 1,000 employees, top dealer with all the manufacturers that he represents — and still growing. Imagine that: At his age, he's still growing, still passionate enough to want to open up another dealership here or there, get another franchise here or there, get bigger, get better. There are very few people who have that type of burning desire."

That lesson has rubbed off on a lot of people I've worked with over the years — not just Rick Case associates.

"That's what Rick does — he thinks big," Tom Gruber says. "And every time he thinks big, he thinks, 'Well, I'm going to think even bigger next time.' And he does. The best lesson I've learned from Rick is to never think small. Think as big as you can and then go for it.

"In his own mind, there are no boundaries. He can accomplish anything. He keeps going back after it until he gets it done. No matter what it takes or how long it takes, he believes he is going to be No. 1 — and he believes it so fully to the point that other people believe it. And if they believe it, they're so much more able to accomplish it."

The most successful people get to where they are because they're never satisfied with the last level of success they accomplished. They always believe that they can be better and achieve more. That has always been — and will always be — our philosophy of moving forward at Rick Case. Other dealers would be content to say, "Look at what we've already achieved." They think it seems too difficult to push themselves further and accomplish more things that seem impossible. But that's the only way you get to be No. 1. If your desire is to really come out on top, you will keep pushing yourself further. You have to.

Rick Case smart Center Weston opened January, 2008

The first smart cars arrived January, 2008. Rick, Rita, Tara Stricklin, general manager and Ryan Case, parts and service manager

Raquel Case Studio Manager celebrates the opening of Rick Case Fiat, July 2011

Chrysler Group LLC
CIMS 485-96-16
1000 Chrysler Drive
Auburn Hills, MI USA 48326

One

August 18, 2011

Dear Rick Case,

On behalf of the FIAT Brand North America, we would like to personally congratulate you for your outstanding sales performance in July. Your energy, enthusiasm, and hard work allowed you to become the top selling FIAT studio in the nation your first month in business. We appreciate the tremendous efforts of you and your entire team.

We look forward to a successful collective future.

Sincerely,

Laura J. Soave
Head of FIAT Brand North America

Patrick Dougherty
Director - FIAT Brand Sales North America

Letter of congratulations from Fiat for being #1 in the U.S.

SocialSeen

Rick Case Automotive Group celebrated the grand opening of Rick Case FIAT on June 28, 2011 in Weston. More than 100 guests previewed the new showroom and an extensive inventory of the all new 2012 FIAT 500. Guests took part in the official red-ribbon cutting with Mayor Judy Paul of the town of Davie and were able to compare the all new 2012 FIAT 500 to an older, classic FIAT to see firsthand how the brand has evolved.

The Rick Case FIAT team at the all new Rick Case FIAT dealership

Mayor Judy Paul of the town of Davie and City of Weston Commissioner Jim Norton, with Jack "JJ" Jackintelle, President and Chief Operating Officer of the Rick Case Automotive Group, and Raquel Case, Rick Case FIAT Studio Director

Jasmine Prchal, Scott Herman

Teresa Farina, Jeff Strauss, Raquel Case, Bob Broderdorf Jr.

Gina Manfredi and Georgia Beasley

Raquel Case, FIAT Studio Director, Bob Broderdorf Jr. and Michelle Simon, Publisher of THINK Magazine

Rick Case FIAT

Fiat Grand Opening Think Magazine 8-11 – Article featuring Fiat's grand opening celebration, June 28, 2011

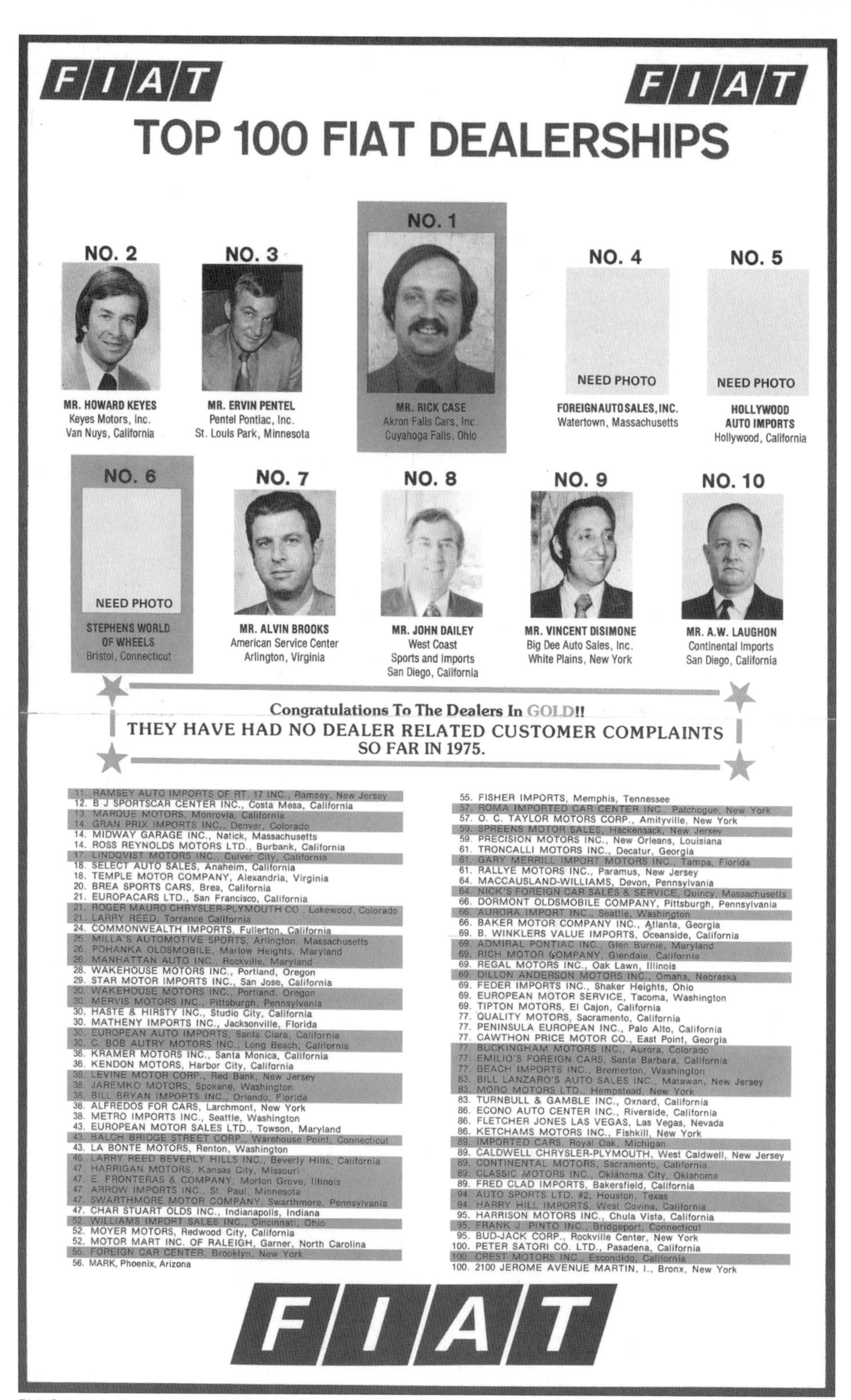

FIAT

FIAT

TOP 100 FIAT DEALERSHIPS

NO. 1
MR. RICK CASE
Akron Falls Cars, Inc.
Cuyahoga Falls, Ohio

NO. 2
MR. HOWARD KEYES
Keyes Motors, Inc.
Van Nuys, California

NO. 3
MR. ERVIN PENTEL
Pentel Pontiac, Inc.
St. Louis Park, Minnesota

NO. 4
NEED PHOTO
FOREIGN AUTO SALES, INC.
Watertown, Massachusetts

NO. 5
NEED PHOTO
HOLLYWOOD AUTO IMPORTS
Hollywood, California

NO. 6
NEED PHOTO
STEPHENS WORLD OF WHEELS
Bristol, Connecticut

NO. 7
MR. ALVIN BROOKS
American Service Center
Arlington, Virginia

NO. 8
MR. JOHN DAILEY
West Coast Sports and Imports
San Diego, California

NO. 9
MR. VINCENT DISIMONE
Big Dee Auto Sales, Inc.
White Plains, New York

NO. 10
MR. A.W. LAUGHON
Continental Imports
San Diego, California

Congratulations To The Dealers In GOLD!!
THEY HAVE HAD NO DEALER RELATED CUSTOMER COMPLAINTS SO FAR IN 1975.

11. RAMSEY AUTO IMPORTS OF RT. 17 INC., Ramsey, New Jersey
12. B J SPORTSCAR CENTER INC., Costa Mesa, California
13. MARQUE MOTORS, Monrovia, California
14. GRAN PRIX IMPORTS INC., Denver, Colorado
14. MIDWAY GARAGE INC., Natick, Massachusetts
14. ROSS REYNOLDS MOTORS LTD., Burbank, California
17. LINDQVIST MOTORS INC., Culver City, California
18. SELECT AUTO SALES, Anaheim, California
18. TEMPLE MOTOR COMPANY, Alexandria, Virginia
20. BREA SPORTS CARS, Brea, California
21. EUROPACARS LTD., San Francisco, California
21. ROGER MAURO CHRYSLER-PLYMOUTH CO., Lakewood, Colorado
21. LARRY REED, Torrance California
24. COMMONWEALTH IMPORTS, Fullerton, California
25. MILLA'S AUTOMOTIVE SPORTS, Arlington, Massachusetts
26. POHANKA OLDSMOBILE, Marlow Heights, Maryland
26. MANHATTAN AUTO INC., Rockville, Maryland
28. WAKEHOUSE MOTORS INC., Portland, Oregon
29. STAR MOTOR IMPORTS INC., San Jose, California
30. WAKEHOUSE MOTORS INC., Portland, Oregon
30. MERVIS MOTORS INC., Pittsburgh, Pennsylvania
30. HASTE & HIRSTY INC., Studio City, California
30. MATHENY IMPORTS INC., Jacksonville, Florida
30. EUROPEAN AUTO IMPORTS, Santa Clara, California
30. C. BOB AUTRY MOTORS INC., Long Beach, California
36. KRAMER MOTORS INC., Santa Monica, California
36. KENDON MOTORS, Harbor City, California
38. LEVINE MOTOR CORP., Red Bank, New Jersey
38. JAREMKO MOTORS, Spokane, Washington
38. BILL BRYAN IMPORTS INC., Orlando, Florida
38. ALFREDOS FOR CARS, Larchmont, New York
38. METRO IMPORTS INC., Seattle, Washington
43. EUROPEAN MOTOR SALES LTD., Towson, Maryland
43. BALCH BRIDGE STREET CORP., Warehouse Point, Connecticut
43. LA BONTE MOTORS, Renton, Washington
46. LARRY REED BEVERLY HILLS INC., Beverly Hills, California
47. HARRIGAN MOTORS, Kansas City, Missouri
47. E. FRONTERAS & COMPANY, Morton Grove, Illinois
47. ARROW IMPORTS INC., St. Paul, Minnesota
47. SWARTHMORE MOTOR COMPANY, Swarthmore, Pennsylvania
47. CHAR STUART OLDS INC., Indianapolis, Indiana
52. WILLIAMS IMPORT SALES INC., Cincinnati, Ohio
52. MOYER MOTORS, Redwood City, California
52. MOTOR MART INC. OF RALEIGH, Garner, North Carolina
55. FOREIGN CAR CENTER, Brooklyn, New York
56. MARK, Phoenix, Arizona
55. FISHER IMPORTS, Memphis, Tennessee
57. ROMA IMPORTED CAR CENTER INC., Patchogue, New York
57. O. C. TAYLOR MOTORS CORP., Amityville, New York
59. SPREENS MOTOR SALES, Hackensack, New Jersey
59. PRECISION MOTORS INC., New Orleans, Louisiana
61. TRONCALLI MOTORS INC., Decatur, Georgia
61. GARY MERRILL IMPORT MOTORS INC., Tampa, Florida
61. RALLYE MOTORS INC., Paramus, New Jersey
64. MACCAUSLAND-WILLIAMS, Devon, Pennsylvania
64. NICK'S FOREIGN CAR SALES & SERVICE, Quincy, Massachusetts
66. DORMONT OLDSMOBILE COMPANY, Pittsburgh, Pennsylvania
66. AURORA IMPORT INC., Seattle, Washington
66. BAKER MOTOR COMPANY INC., Atlanta, Georgia
69. B. WINKLERS VALUE IMPORTS, Oceanside, California
69. ADMIRAL PONTIAC INC., Glen Burnie, Maryland
69. RICH MOTOR COMPANY, Glendale, California
69. REGAL MOTORS INC., Oak Lawn, Illinois
69. DILLON ANDERSON MOTORS INC., Omaha, Nebraska
69. FEDER IMPORTS INC., Shaker Heights, Ohio
69. EUROPEAN MOTOR SERVICE, Tacoma, Washington
69. TIPTON MOTORS, El Cajon, California
77. QUALITY MOTORS, Sacramento, California
77. PENINSULA EUROPEAN INC., Palo Alto, California
77. CAWTHON PRICE MOTOR CO., East Point, Georgia
77. BUCKINGHAM MOTORS INC., Aurora, Colorado
77. EMILIO'S FOREIGN CARS, Santa Barbara, California
77. BEACH IMPORTS INC., Bremerton, Washington
83. BILL LANZARO'S AUTO SALES INC., Matawan, New Jersey
83. MORO MOTORS LTD., Hempstead, New York
83. TURNBULL & GAMBLE INC., Oxnard, California
86. ECONO AUTO CENTER INC., Riverside, California
86. FLETCHER JONES LAS VEGAS, Las Vegas, Nevada
86. KETCHAMS MOTORS INC., Fishkill, New York
89. IMPORTED CARS, Royal Oak, Michigan
89. CALDWELL CHRYSLER-PLYMOUTH, West Caldwell, New Jersey
89. CONTINENTAL MOTORS, Sacramento, California
89. CLASSIC MOTORS INC., Oklahoma City, Oklahoma
89. FRED CLAD IMPORTS, Bakersfield, California
94. AUTO SPORTS LTD. #2, Houston, Texas
94. HARRY HILL IMPORTS, West Covina, California
95. HARRISON MOTORS INC., Chula Vista, California
95. FRANK J. PINTO INC., Bridgeport, Connecticut
95. BUD-JACK CORP., Rockville Center, New York
100. PETER SATORI CO. LTD., Pasadena, California
100. CREST MOTORS INC., Escondido, California
100. 2100 JEROME AVENUE MARTIN, I., Bronx, New York

FIAT

Rick Case is the largest volume Fiat dealer in the country, with the highest customer satisfaction index, 1975.

The Next Chapter

The 50th Anniversary Celebration

Rita and I and the rest of our team are tremendously proud of what we've achieved over the last 50 years. But our idea of success doesn't rest in the company — it stretches out to the community. That's why we decided to celebrate the 50th anniversary of the Rick Case Auto Group in January 2012 by benefiting the entire community.

It's really not a party for Rick Case as much as it's a party by Rick Case for the community. For this event, we selected a theme that's bigger than our business by asking, "When I opened my first car dealership in 1962, what else was happening that people cared about?"

It was exciting to discover that The Beach Boys were recording their first album and somewhere in Liverpool, The Beatles were getting together. Why not celebrate it all, we thought, with a 60s-themed party featuring the best Beatles tribute band we could find — BeatleMania from New York — and the best Beach Boys tribute band we could find — Papa Doo Run Run from California.

Our goal was to celebrate our 50th year as a car dealer for the benefit of our community and make it a party that would be memorable for many years to come. We invited more than 20 charities to be the beneficiaries of 100 percent of the proceeds raised from our celebration. We are underwriting the entire cost and planning every detail. The charities only have to recruit their supporters to become sponsors, and 100 percent of the proceeds will benefit their organizations. We secured the biggest venue in the community — The Signature Grand in Davie, Florida, which holds more than 1,200 people — for this "50 Years of Rockin' & Rollin'" celebration. This event was designed to be all about the community — not just about Rita and Rick Case and the Rick Case Auto Group.

"This 50th anniversary project — I've never heard of any concept like that that involves so many charities," Tom Gruber says. "This is very innovative because Rick and Rita funded the whole thing and paid for everything themselves. So 100 percent of what anybody contributes benefits many different charities."

The other way we made the anniversary event all about the community was by making it a learning experience for the charities involved. Instead of presenting what would be a one-off experience, we wanted something with inherent takeaway value. In June 2011, when we announced the party, we told the charities involved that we wanted to share our 25 years of South Florida charity event experience with them. That meant taking the time to teach our beneficiaries how this event was being assembled and how each charity can achieve the same type of results with their future events that we have achieved with ours. They received ideas on how to bring in auction items, how to manage live and silent auctions, how to gain celebrity support, and more importantly, how persistence removes resistance in selling sponsorships and tickets.

We even built an entire website for the event at www.RickCase50th.com to keep the whole community connected to us as the party approached.

No one has ever done an event like this before. CEOs of major companies in Broward County called us to say, "We can't believe it. This is so creative. Why didn't anyone think of this before? You've got the whole community rallied around celebrating your 50th anniversary for the benefit of the community."

The reason no one thought of this before is because no one else stopped to ask: Who else could benefit from our 50th anniversary? To us, it was common sense to celebrate 50 years in business by giving back to the communities that supported our business and made our success possible.

SOCIALSEEN

What do The Beatles, The Beach Boys, and the Rick Case Automotive Group have in common? Fifty years of success!

And as a tribute to this tremendous milestone Rita and Rick Case hosted a unique charity benefit. The event benefitted 21 different charities and coined 50 years of Rockin' & Rollin'

Photos courtesy of Robert Stolpe

Rita and Rick Case
(Photo courtesy of Dream Focus Photography)

Stacy Ostrau from Sun Sentinel Children's Fund, and Mark Snead from PACE Center for Girls Broward

Rita and Rick Case with the representatives from the 21 charity participants

Maureen Hodrot and Amy Cassini, from Habitat for Humanity Broward, with Marcy Falcone from SOS Children's Villages - Florida

Rick Case with Arlene Pecora from The Signature Grand and Rita Case

Sharon Ellington from 4KIDS of South Florida with Susan DeYoung from Habitat for Humanity Broward

Mary Falcone from SOS Children's Villages – Florida and Valerie Zucker, CEO and Founder of Zucker Public Relations

Kerry Becker and Brian Quail of the Boys & Girls Clubs of Broward County, with Fonda Huizenga from 4KIDS of South Florida

88

Kickoff for charity event to celebrate the 50th anniversary of Rick Case's first car dealership

Epilogue

The future for Rick Case

If the past 50 years have been any kind of indicator for the rest of this century, then the Rick Case Auto Group will keep breaking records as we break new ground. We will keep growing because that's the only option. In any business, if all you do is hold steady or tread water, you'll start to fall behind very quickly. You must move forward if you intend to stay competitive and be successful in any business. That has always been the driving force behind our success. No matter how many cars we sell or how big we become, we're never satisfied. This philosophy permeates our organization.

When you keep raising the bar and adding new projects to the mix, you keep yourself motivated. I suppose if you do the same thing day after day, year after year, you will become bored and complacent. But when you challenge yourself and raise your definition of success, you will continuously inspire and motivate yourself. Unless you challenge yourself to do more and go further than you already have, you will never grow or improve.

At the Rick Case Auto Group, we are always looking for the next opportunity, thinking about the next big idea, and setting the bar higher. Entrepreneurs are never content with success. They view a win as a reason to push themselves to become even more successful. For me, this means asking questions like, "How can we be the first? How can we be the best? How can we be the biggest?" By pushing yourself to take things up a notch every year, you'll find additional growth opportunities. That's why the Rick Case Auto Group will be better and bigger and break more records in the next 50 years than we have so far.

We recognize that in order to achieve long-term success, you can't build a business on selling just cars. That's why I tell my associates that we're not in the car business — we're in the relationship business. If you sell a car, you sell one. If you build a relationship, you sell many. We wouldn't have made it 50 years if our only objective was to just sell cars. When you focus on the customer first, the business will follow. I can't stress it enough: Treat every customer as you would your best friend instead of seeing each person as just another sale. With this as the cornerstone of our business, we continue to bring in traffic and build loyalty with our customers. This keeps our business growing and secure as we look toward the next 50 years.

When I look to the future, I see much more than simply a thriving company. I envision a thriving community around it. Where other dealers would have been content to sit back and say, "I've got 15 dealerships," we stood up and reached for more. Being successful in business is not enough; we want to share our success by giving back to the communities that have supported us and by helping children find better futures than the ones they're dealt.

In both business and philanthropy, our philosophy is to always keep reaching further and setting our goals higher — whether that means selling more cars or raising more money for a cause. Once you set a goal, don't let anything keep you from reaching it. Once you reach a goal, don't sit around gloating over it. Set another target and then pursue it.

Brian Quail, CEO of the Boys & Girls Clubs of Broward County, paints the picture this way:

"At the end of last year's Concours d'Elegance, as we stood on the show field presenting the last award on that Sunday, I thanked Rick and Rita for what they did to help us carry off such a wonderful event that raised the most money ever in the world for a charity at an automotive event. As we shook hands, he looked at me and said, 'Well, I guess we have to start planning for next year.' Here we are enjoying the success of a wonderful weekend, and there he is, already talking about how to improve it. That states the type of person he is: While you can achieve great success, you never can be satisfied with that success; you keep needing to raise the bar."

From the Boys & Girls Clubs' perspective, the goals are straightforward: Make each event bigger and better than ever, raising more money to improve the lives of more children. That's been a common theme for me in both business and philanthropy. I believe that the only way you stay successful is by achieving more success. And the only way you do that is by setting each goal higher than the one before. When I say, "Well done," you can expect one of the next things out of my mouth to be, "What next?"

"It was the fifth year of the Concours last year, and he kept saying it was going to be bigger than ever," Kerry Becker remembers. "We had 2,000 the year before on Sunday. We had 7,500 people come through the gates last year. I did not believe that he would get that many people there.

"The event's not even halfway over and he comes up to me and says, 'Well, let's start talking about next year.' I couldn't believe it. That's just how he's thinking: 'It's a huge success. We've got room for improvement on this. How can we make this better? How can I top this? What's my wow factor?' That's how he is. He'll say, 'Great job,' and then 10 minutes later, 'OK, how can we make it greater?'"

There's a reason why I have worked so hard to spark in others this sense of never being satisfied with success. When you get everyone around you saying, "We achieved this, now what's next?" you perpetuate success. You set it in motion so that people keep striving to be the best, even without you telling them to do so. In my case, it was important to make day-to-day operations sustainable under our president, Jack Jackintelle, so I could take a step back to focus on acquiring new franchises, building new dealerships, and charity events. We have worked very carefully to put a team in place that will carry out our vision for day-to-day operations of the dealerships while Rita and I focus on growing the company and giving back to the community.

"We want to keep the culture that has made the company successful, from the fact that every single customer has our cell phone numbers to treating every customer as our best friend," Jackintelle continues. "I reassure him that we keep the culture going because it's just in the walls."

A big benefit of having a younger management team is that they can balance the legacy of culture with the changes necessary to adapt and modernize our business for today's environment. That balance is crucial for managing any organization into the future.

"Rick's a traditionalist," Jackintelle says. "He recognized that he needed Gen-X leaders to be able to manage the new generation of associates, which are 18- to 30-year-olds in Gen-Y. He needed someone in my generation to be able to do things that are done differently today than they were 40 years ago.

"His intensity is so over the top, and he recognizes that sometimes it just freaks people out. I try to take that intensity and package it up in a way that this younger generation can understand. The expectations and the end results are still the same, but he allows me to communicate it when and how it works for them."

That's why we've been adamant about training to pave the way for the future of the Rick Case Auto Group. We've invested a lot in our process of hiring and developing associates by sharing our technical know-how and customer-focused culture. Training is a way of sustaining success for the long term.

That's true for future of the charity events I've developed, as well. I've made similar efforts in philanthropy to get the right people involved who have the combination of care and capability to support the cause into the future.

When we talk about the future, we get a lot of questions about our children and how they factor into our succession planning. In many family-owned businesses, especially dealerships, children are brought up in the company and groomed to one day take the reins from their parents. Rita is a prime example of that tradition, starting in her parents' dealership by doing office work and then eventually working her way up to general manager.

But we never brought Ryan and Raquel into our business that way — partly because of timing. By the time our children were old enough to be any help at the store, our company had grown too big. We had become a multiple dealership group with a management company — a rare set-up for car dealerships at the time. There was really no place for them to get started like there would have been in a single-dealership operation. Besides, we didn't want to assume that Ryan or Raquel would want to grow into assigned roles. We want them to make their own career decisions.

They have both tried different endeavors over the years — with stints as a chef here or a telemarketer there. After college, both of our children decided they wanted to work at our company. But they have always worked with our management — never directly with Rita or me. While many dealers build their succession plans around their children, our succession plan isn't predetermined — because our children's careers are theirs to determine.

Raquel is already very successful heading up our newest Fiat dealership in Davie, Florida, where she became the largest dealer in the country our first month in business, setting a new all-time national sales record. She has already drawn comments about her similarities to her mother — both in appearance and sales results. Ryan is also very successful with our company as the general manager of the Honda Powerhouse dealership that sells Honda motorcycles and power products in Davie, Florida. His dealership holds the national one-month Honda motorcycle sales record. They both have the tools they need to be at the front of Rick Case's future success — but then again, so do all of our associates, because we've trained them all equally.

The other question we're frequently asked is where our future growth plans lie. We feel there's still plenty of potential with fast-growing franchises in our current markets. To go into a new market where nobody's ever heard of Rick Case would be very expensive to build our brand. Today, it's much easier, more efficient, and more productive to focus on strengthening our brand, driving it deeper into the markets where we are successfully established. We want to maximize the opportunity we have in our current markets.

It is amazing how much opportunity there is today, considering the changes and the challenges we've experienced in the retail car industry. In just one year, 2009, General Motors and Chrysler went bankrupt, thousands of dealers went out of business, and brands like Pontiac, Saturn, Mercury, and Hummer disappeared. Now, the future looks great for the dealers and brands that remain with the huge, pent-up demand that exists today for new cars.

When I first started my business, the market consisted only of domestic cars. There weren't really any European cars here. Now, more than half of the business is composed of import cars from Europe, Japan, and Korea. I was one of the pioneers at the helm of this change, and was successful for two main reasons: First, I pursued import brands that I was confident in because they were high-quality, fuel-efficient, low-cost cars that would appeal to the masses and sell in high volume. Second, I came up with creative promotions to make consumers more comfortable buying these import brands.

New and different products will keep coming out, accelerated by technology, and it can be difficult to know where to focus your company's attention — whether you're a manufacturer, a distributor, or, like us, a retailer. Those decisions actually become easy when you have a defined focus and you know what you want to become and how you are going to get there. For us, that meant identifying the traits that would make a franchise popular with consumers, accomplishing two things: building customer loyalty and increasing sales. Because we know which traits to look for, we have a successful formula for acquiring new franchises and making acquisitions.

The biggest change that will impact every business in the future, including ours, is the consumers' expectations. I have seen this shift considerably over the past 50 years, altered in part by the other changes going on in terms of products and competition. The key to navigating this change is simple: When you treat every customer like you would your best friend, you keep meeting their needs even as those needs change. The easiest way to prepare for the future is building a relationship with your customer today.

Today's consumers are so much more demanding than people who bought cars in the 1970s and '80s — they demand great service, personal attention, and convenience to retain their loyalty. They look for transparent policies — such as free trial periods with money-back guarantees, maximum term warranties, and full disclosure of finance and leasing terms — as well as transparent communication tools such as social media. These demands have revolutionized the thought process for marketing, advertising, and selling products.

Fortunately for me, these demands — great service, personal attention, and convenience — have always been a foundation of my business since the beginning. We've always treated each customer as our best friend by handing out our home and cell phone numbers and innovating new services, benefits, guarantees, and rewards to give customers what they want. Customers are what really build a business, so when you focus on meeting their needs, you will always succeed.

There will always be new challenges in every business, but if you're creative and passionate, then you will keep creating new ways to overcome those challenges and succeed. The dealerships and other businesses that survive and even thrive throughout the rest of this century will be the ones who are able to change before they're forced to react to change. The people behind these companies will recognize that and eagerly participate in developing the new ideas that drive change. They will be the pioneers of the 21st century. And if by reading this book you become one of those pioneers, then I will have accomplished my goal in writing this book.

The End

Vol. 16 No. 8
August 2009

Dealer
magazine

Ryan Case

Raquel Case

Rick Case

Jim Ziegler:
When the Blitz is On
page 10

Leadership:
Culture Check-up: Do You Have a High Performance Business Culture?
page 14

Ownership:
Franchise Opportunities – Post Wind-down
page 18

Advertising:
The 30-Second Ad Challenge
page 59

Fixed Operations:
Is it Worth Three Bucks a Minute?
page 66

RICK CASE
Rick Case Automotive Group
page 22

Rita Case

Dealer
page 27

Recognition & Achievement Awards

2011 Rita and Rick Case honored as Entrepreneurs of the Year by Ernst & Young

2011 Rita and Rick Case honored as Outstanding Business Leader by Northwood University

2011 Rita and Rick Case presented the 2010 Honda President's Award
- Largest dealer in the country to ever receive this award 3 years in a row -

2011 Rita and Rick Case honored as Humanitarian of the Year by the Soref Jewish Community Center

2010 Rita Case honored as Top 100 Leading Women in the North American Automotive Industry
by Automotive News

2008 Rita and Rick Case presented with Style and Substance Award by Symphony of the Americas

2007 Rita and Rick Case honored as Outstanding Philanthropist by the Association of Fundraising Professionals

2007 Rick Case Auto Group honored as Outstanding Corporate Philanthropist
by the Association of Fundraising Professionals

2007 Rita Case presented Spirit of Leadership Award
at the National Automotive Dealers Association Convention by the Women's Automobile Association

2006 Rita and Rick Case honored as Leaders of the Year by Leadership Broward Foundation

2006 Rita and Rick Case presented the Dealer Education Award by Northwood University

2006 Rita and Rick Case inducted into the Business Hall of Fame by Junior Achievement of South Florida

2006 Rick Case presented with the Time Magazine Dealer of the Year Award

2005 Rita and Rick Case presented with the Valor Award by the American Diabetes Association

2005 Rita Case named Distinguished Woman of the Year by Northwood University

2004 Rita and Rick Case presented in New York City the USA Today and the National Automobile
Dealer Asociation 2003 National Dealer Innovation Award

2004 Rick Case presented the Rotary International "Paul Harris Fellow" Award

2003 Rita and Rick Case presented the South Florida Sun-Sentinel Excalibur Award

2003 Rita and Rick Case presented Humanitarian of the Year Award by EASE Foundation

2003 Rita and Rick Case presented Humanitarian of the Year Award by Nova Southeastern University

2001 Rick Case inducted into the Entrepreneurial Hall of Fame of Nova Southeastern University Wayne Huizenga
Graduate School of Business and Entrepreneurship.

2000 Rita and Rick Case presented the Boys and Girls Clubs Dream Makers Award for over 10 years of service and
donating over $1 Million. (This award has been presented to only 3 other honorees in 15 years)

1999 Rick Case presented the Silver Medallion Award by the Boys and Girls Clubs of America

(continued)

Recognition & Achievement Awards (Continued)

1997 Rick Case received the AIADA Sports Illustrated All-Star Dealer Award in Washington D.C. for demonstrating outstanding customer service, community service and leadership within the Automotive Industry.

1996 Rick Case presented the Child Advocate of the Year Award by Child Care Connection.

1996 Rick Case presented the Bronze Keystone Award by Boys and Girls Clubs of America.

1995 Rick Case presented the C.A.R.E. Award – (Children Are Reasons for Excellence) by the Boys and Girls Clubs of America and Florida Area Council.

1993 Rick Case presented the "Rick Case" Pinnacle Award which was created to recognize extraordinary dedication to the Boys and Girls Clubs.

1988 Rick Case presented with the Star Achievement Award by the Boys and Girls Clubs of Broward County

- BOARD PARTICIPATION - RICK CASE

Boys and Girls Clubs of Broward County Corporate Board, 1986 –present

Boys and Girls Clubs Executive Committee, 1996 - 2008

Boys and Girls Clubs Chairman, 1998

Boys and Girls Clubs President, 1996 & 1997

Boys and Girls Clubs - Founding President New Davie Clubs 2002

Boys and Girls Clubs Co-President of Davie, Florida Club 2002-2006 with wife Rita Case

Broward Workshop Board Broward County Economic Advisors 2000-present

The Broward Alliance CEO Council 2008-present

Board of Trustees Nova Southeastern University 2002-present

Broward County Sheriff's Advisory Board 2003-present

Plantation Gateway Community Redevelopment Advisory Board 1999-04

- BOARD PARTICIPATION - RITA CASE

Community Foundation of Broward Executive Board, 1999 - 2006

Comerica Bank Advisory Board, 2002 – present

Work Life Balance Institute for Women, 2000 – 2010

Northwood University Distinguished Women's Executive Board, 2007 - present

Northwood University Outstanding Business Leaders Executive Board, 2010 - present

Rick Case Bikes for Kids, Founder, 1982 – present
Donated bicycles are brought to Rick Case Dealerships and through the Boys and Girls Clubs and other charities are distributed to needy Children every Christmas. Originated in Ohio in 1982, spread to Florida and Georgia

Boys and Girls Clubs Showboats International Rendezvous - Founder and Producer, 1988 - present
Three-day event for mega-yacht owners

Boys and Girls Clubs Ft. Lauderdale International Auto Show - Founder 1990 - present
All proceeds benefit the Boys and Girls Clubs

Admiral's Club - Founder, 1994 - present
Members donate $50,000 a year to the Boys & Girls Clubs at the annual Boys and Girls Club Showboats International Rendezvous

Boys and Girls Clubs Ship' n' Shore - Founder, 1995 – 2005
Progressive party on the Ft. Lauderdale waterways touring million dollar homes and mega-yachts that are for sale.

Boys and Girls Clubs Bikers Ball - Founder, 1995 – 2005
Three day motorcycle event during Bike Week in Daytona Beach

Boys and Girls Clubs WestFair - Founder, 1996 – 2001

Boys and Girls Clubs $20 Million Dollar Capital Campaign - President, 1996 & 1997
Raised $22.4 Million

Boys and Girls Clubs Ranch Roam - Founder, 1996 - present
An annual western evening event with up to 1,000 participants a year on a real working ranch

Boys and Girls Clubs Bikers Bash - Founder, 1998 – present
Three day motorcycle event in Fort Lauderdale

The Leader of the Pack Club - Founder, 1998 - present
Members donate $5,000 a year to the Boys and Girls Clubs at annual Bikers Bash

Cattlemen's Club - Founder, 1998 – present
Members donate $5,000 a year to the Boys and Girls Clubs at annual Ranch Roam

Rick and Rita Case Boys and Girls Club - Opened in Davie, Florida 2003

Boys and Girls Clubs Grand Oakes Caddy Shack Revisited - Founder, 2003 - present
Annual Golf Tournament

The Admiral's Boys and Girls Clubs Marine Academy - Founder, 2004 - present
At-risk youth training for marine-industry careers

Boys & Girls Clubs Boca Raton Concours d'Elegance - Founder and Producer, 2007 - present
3-Day Classic Car Event at the Boca Raton Resort & Club

Big Wheels Club - Founder, 2007-present
Members donate $10,000 a year to the Boys and Girls Clubs at the Boca Raton Concours d'Elegance

Rick Case Honda, Davie, Florida

Rick Case Hyundai, Roswell, Georgia

Rick Case Fiat, Davie, Florida

Rick Case Audi, Atlanta, Georgia

Rick Case Acura, Fort Lauderdale, Florida

Rick Case Hyundai, Bedford, Ohio

Rick Case Mistubishi, Bedford, Ohio

Rick Case Hyundai, Atlanta, Georgia

Rick Case, Honda, Cleveland, Ohio

Rick Case Hyundai, Davie, Florida

Rick Case Hyundai, Cleveland, Ohio

Rick Case Hyundai, Fort Lauderdale, Florida

Rick Case Kia, Atlanta, Georgia

Rick Case Powerhouse Honda Motorcycles, Davie, Florida